Kind Regards

'Sir, more than kisses, letters mingle souls; for, thus friends absent speak.'

– John Donne

Kind Regards

THE LOST ART OF

LETTER-WRITING

LIZ WILLIAMS

Michael O'Mara Books Limited

First published in Great Britain in 2012 by
Michael O'Mara Books Limited
9 Lion Yard
Tremadoc Road
London SW4 7NQ

ISBN: 978-1-84317-713-5 in hardback print format
ISBN: 978-1-84317-920-7 in EPub format
ISBN: 978-1-84317-919-1 in Mobipocket format

1 2 3 4 5 6 7 8 9 10

Designed and typeset by K DESIGN, Winscombe, Somerset
Illustrations by Andrew Pinder
Printed and bound in Great Britain by Clays Ltd, St Ives plc

www.mombooks.com

Contents

Foreword

Dear reader,

What is a letter? The dictionary says this:

Letter (noun) – a written or printed communication directed to a person or organization, usually sent by post in an envelope.

But a letter is more, so much more. We have been writing letters to one another since around the fourth millennium BC and, while email and the telephone may make letter-writing less essential than before, I firmly believe we will continue to put pen to paper for the foreseeable future.

Letters provide a form of time travelling – they bridge the years in ink. I felt a sense of awe at reading the thoughts of those who experienced the pivotal moments in history – the fall of Rome, the start of a 'small cult' called Christianity, the eve of the Second World War, the threat of the Cold War.

They also give an insight into the everyday life, emotions, hopes, dreams, expectations, loves and disappointments of our forebears. They show that we have more in common with our distant ancestors than we might imagine.

How can you not love letters? I have boxes of old letters – and every so often I take them out, unfold them and re-read them. They remind me of the person I once was; the loves and losses I have suffered over the years; my own personal history captured in ink.

Researching this book was at times a very emotional experience. I knew many of the great letter-writers, but others came as delectable surprises. Tender love letters stole my heart. The tragic last letters from people facing death brought a lump to my throat. The correspondence between parents of sick or dying children made the mother in me weep.

Psychotherapists believe that writing letters – honestly and from the heart – acts as a powerful form of self-therapy; that it can bring clarity and a means of expressing emotions. Can you do that with an email? Perhaps. But somehow the act of putting pen to paper gives a further depth and meaning to the words.

In this book I didn't just want to reproduce great letters – I wanted to investigate the whole subject of letter-writing: the materials that have been used over the millennia; the history of letter-writing and of the post; the curious and inventive forms of the letter that have emerged over the years. I also wanted to remind the reader how to construct letters for all occasions, with advice on how to set out both formal and informal letters.

And so I fell in love with letters all over again. As the Reverend T. Cooke asserts in *The Universal Letter Writer*, 'Letters are the trade of life – the fuel of love – the pleasure of friendship – the food of the politician and the entertainment of the curious. To speak to those we love or esteem, is the greatest satisfaction we are capable of knowing; and the next is, being able to converse with them by letter.'

I hope you gain as much pleasure from reading this book as I did in writing it. And, please, let's all do our bit to keep the gentle art of letter-writing alive.

Yours truly,

Liz Williams

PART ONE

*From
Paper to Post*

Dear reader: introducing the letter

A letter is a written or printed communication directed to a person or organization, usually sent by post in an envelope. The modern English word 'letter' comes from the Old French *lettre* that, in turn, derives from the Latin *littera*, meaning letter of the alphabet. *Littera* could also mean writing, a document or record, and in its plural form *litterae*, an epistle. The first recorded usage of this sense is in the early thirteenth century.

The word 'missive' derives from the medieval Latin *missivus*, which comes from the verb *mittere* – 'to send'.

Definitions

Epistle (noun) – a letter, especially a formal one.
A literary composition in the form of a letter.

Epistolographic (adjective) – pertaining to the
writing of letters; used in writing letters; epistolary.
Epistolographic character of writing.

Why letter-writing began

Writing letters most likely began when ancient cultures
expanded their political and economic stretch. They
would have needed reliable means for transmitting
information, maintaining financial accounts, keeping
historical records, and so forth. What seems certain is
that around 4,000 BC trade and administration started
becoming simply too complex to rely solely on the
power of memory. So writing became a more depend-
able method of recording, sending and presenting
transactions in a permanent form.

In both Mesoamerica and Ancient Egypt writing
may have evolved through calendrics: historical and
environmental events that needed to be recorded.

What letters are called around the world

رسالة	(Arabic)
Писмо	(Bulgarian)
信	(Chinese)
Dopis	(Czech)
Brief	(Dutch)
Sulat	(Filipino)
Kirje	(Finnish)
Lettre	(French)
Schreiben	(German)
Επιστολή	(Greek)
בתכמ	(Hebrew)
Surat	(Indonesian)
Lettera	(Italian)
手紙	(Japanese)
편지	(Korean)
List	(Polish)
Письмо	(Russian)
Carta	(Spanish)
Barua	(Swahili)
Skrivelse	(Swedish)
Llythyr	(Welsh)

Why you should write letters

With the advent of instant messaging and a continual rise in postal costs, the handwritten letter can often seem both primitive and expensive. Yet the coldness of the keyboard can little compare to the warmth and familiarity of receiving a physical letter. Whether well written or not, the letter offers a human connection, as these great writers testify.

★ 'To send a letter is a good way to go somewhere without moving anything but your heart.'
    – PHYLLIS THEROUX

★ 'Letter-writing is the only device for combining solitude with good company.' – LORD BYRON

★ 'The art of art, the glory of expression and the sunshine of the light of letters, is simplicity.'
    – WALT WHITMAN

★ 'In our letters we are recollecting and conversing with the soul, through both our friends and ourselves.' – THOMAS MOORE

★ 'A single paragraph in an impulsive letter will often tell more about a man than a whole work calculated by him to the same ostensible end.'
– GEORGE JEAN NATHAN

★ 'Life would split apart without letters.'
– VIRGINIA WOOLF

Erasmus

Desiderius Erasmus Roterodamus (1466–1536), usually known as Erasmus of Rotterdam, was a priest, theologian and classical scholar. A humanist, he wrote many books as well as preparing new Latin and Greek editions of the New Testament. He said this of letter-writing:

A letter is a mutual conversation between absent friends, which should be neither unpolished, rough, nor artificial, nor confined to a single topic, nor tediously long. Thus the epistolary form favours simplicity, frankness, humour, and wit.

Dear reader

The first recorded use of 'Dear' as a salutation was in 1250 AD, several hundred years before the advent of printing. While we may have become used to the expression through repeated use, encompassed in the word is a sense of affection and respect – a 'dear friend' is one beloved. This tells us that letter-writing was used from at least this time as a form of intimacy.

But does 'Dear' still have a place in modern letter-writing? Is it at odds with the professional context in which we might receive a letter from a bank manager, or an energy supplier? According to an article from 2010 in *The Wall Street Journal*, 'across the Internet the use of "dear" is going the way of sealing wax,' but there is no question that 'Hey there' or 'Hi' would be too informal in many circumstances. Perhaps for this reason alone it is still used in business, political and legislative contexts.

Putting pen to paper

Letters have been written on a hugely wide variety of materials throughout history, which include stone tablets, clay tablets, wax tablets, vellum, paper, pottery, bones, turtle and tortoise shells, and leaves. The Grecian scholar Cadmus is credited with introducing the first alphabet or Phoenician alphabet, creating characters that then formed the basis of written communication. Paper is thought to have been invented in China in the second century BC and was made from hemp waste, which was soaked and beaten into a pulp with a wooden mallet. The word paper derives from the Latin word *papyrus*, which was a thick paper-like material produced from the *Cyperus papyrus* plant.

On choosing writing materials

With so many writing materials available it can be tricky to decide what to choose for different styles of letter. Jennifer Williams, author of *The Pleasures of Staying in Touch*, gives the following advice.

★   It is best to use plain white, ivory, light blue, or grey stationery (or notecards) for condolence letters, thank-you notes, and replies to formal and informal invitations.

★ For business correspondence, it is customary to send a typed letter on plain white or ivory standard size (8 ½" x 11") paper, with a matching envelope.

★ Indulge your passion for beautiful writing materials: most stationers offer a stunning variety of papers, envelopes, pens, scented inks, and sealing waxes.

★ Sealing wax is making a comeback these days, but unfortunately it sometimes gets crushed at the post office during mechanical processing.

★ Some writers choose irregular sheets of paper and unusually large envelopes for their correspondence, and even send letters rolled up in decorative tubes, bottles, or boxes.

★ Others use their favourite scent to leave a redolent imprint of themselves on the page.

★ Embossing and engraving are excellent, if more traditional, ways to individualize stationery, and, certainly, if you have a family crest, it too can be used to give letters a personal touch.

How to make scented ink

- Blend approximately ten drops of essential oil (rose or lavender are suggested) with a teaspoon of vodka.
- Add the mixture, a little at a time, to a small bottle of ink (deep colours work the best).
- Stir thoroughly and the ink is ready to use.

Dos and Don'ts of preserving letters

Do:

★   Store letters flat in a container out of the light.

★   Handle as little as possible.

★   Avoid staples, paperclips and rubber bands (unless letters are already taped or so on – don't try to undo what has already been done).

★   Store at around seventy degrees or less and in humidity of ideally around forty to fifty per cent. Keep temperature and humidity even.

★   Use 'acid-free' archival folders and boxes.

Don't:

★ Store newspaper clippings with letters –
 newsprint is acidic and may stain the letters.

★ Keep letters in garages, attics or sheds where
 temperatures fluctuate. Keep away from
 radiators, pipes, vents and food.

★ Be tempted to frame or mount letters and don't
 put in scrapbooks.

On not writing letters

Before you begin writing, make sure you have a purpose, even if it is just to say hello to an old friend. An
angry letter written in bitterness or a thoughtless letter
written in haste is likely to be a source of regret if sent.

★ 'Never write a letter if you can help it, and never
 destroy one!' – JOHN A. MACDONALD

★ 'If you are in doubt whether to write a letter or not, don't. And the advice applies to many doubts in life besides that of letter writing.'
– EDWARD BULWER LYTTON

★ 'When a man sends you an impudent letter, sit right down and give it back to him with interest ten times compounded, and then throw both letters in the wastebasket.' – ELBERT HUBBARD

★ 'Letters frighten me more than anything else in life. They contain greater possibilities of murder than any poison. I think you ought only to write to a person when you are in the same place and quite certain to see them. When a letter is a continuation of presence it is alright, but when it becomes a codification of absence it is intolerable.' – ELIZABETH BIBESCO

Post haste: the history of the mail system

'A letter is an unannounced visit, the postman the agent of rude surprises. One ought to reserve an hour a week for receiving letters and afterwards take a bath.'

Friedrich Nietzsche

With global couriers, airmail and complex networks of depots with advanced sorting technology it is now possible to send a letter from one country to another and to have it arrive within a few hours. Yet we still rely on manpower and transport systems, much like the ancients. Thousands of years before the first modern mail systems were put in place, the ancients used couriers, often based on a relay system.

The earliest post

★   In ancient Egypt, the Pharoahs used couriers as far back as 2400 BC.

★   Hammurabi (1792–50 BC), king of Babylon, is said to have established one of the earliest forms of 'postal system'. It worked on having stations (*chapar-khaneh*) where the message carrier (*chapar*) would swap horses. The service was later called *angariae*, from the Greek form of a Babylonian word adopted in Persia to mean 'mounted courier'.

★   The Mauryan Empire, a historical power in ancient India (322–185 BC), developed a mail service with chariots known as *dagana* used to send missives. Runners and even pigeons were also used to distribute post.

★   In China, the postal network of relays of couriers was considerably expanded under the Han dynasty (206 BC–AD 220). The couriers used staging posts about nine miles apart at which to change their mounts.

★ The Romans established the first two-tier mail system. It was known as *cursus publicus*. Light carriages called *rhedae*, pulled by fast horses, were used for the 'first-class' service while two-wheeled carts (*birolae*), pulled by oxen, provided a slower service.

★ Genghis Khan, founder of the Mongol Empire, instigated an empire-wide postal station system named *Ortoo*. By the end of his grandson Kublai Khan's reign this had expanded to encompass more than 1,400 postal stations in China alone, with stations fifteen to forty miles apart.

Pigeon post

From its first known use in ancient Egypt until the invention of the telegraph in 1844, pigeon post was the world's fastest communication system and was essential for intelligence gathering. Employed by news agencies, banks, traders and the military, pigeons have been unparalleled in the relaying of information between parties internationally.

In the Franco-Prussian War of 1870–1, a gap existed in telegraph lines between France and Germany. Julius Reuter bridged it with pigeons and made the fortune he used as the basis of what is now Reuters, one of the world's great news agencies.

During World War I, the British Air Force kept over 20,000 pigeons for a special mission. Each bird was placed inside a basket that was attached to a rigged balloon and a parachute. When the balloons were over enemy territory, the baskets were landed softly by way of the parachutes. A message inside each basket asked the finder to supply intelligence information for a promised reward, and to put the information in the message holder attached to the bird. Once released the pigeon would then fly home to Britain.

The Roman Office of Letters

In ancient Rome there was an imperial chancery, known as the Office of Letters (*ab epistulis*) in which directives, edits, documents and letters were drawn up. It was subdivided into a Greek and a Latin department. By the fifth century there were four letter offices, all of which came under the ultimate control of the *magister officiorum*.

The early British postal system

The 'King's Post' had existed since 1510 and the General Post Office was established in London in 1710. Before Rowland Hill introduced the 'Penny Post', postage depended on how far the letter had to travel and how many sheets of paper it contained. For example, in 1812 the cost for a single letter was 4d (pence) for up to fifteen miles. Sending a letter from London to Brighton would cost 8d; if it went to Nottingham the cost increased to 10d and to send a letter to Edinburgh, Scotland would be a colossal 1 shilling 1½ d (about a day's average salary). If two sheets of paper were used the cost doubled. To add to the irritation, the receiver rather than the sender had to pay the postage – so the Post Office spent a lot of time arguing with reluctant recipients.

Mice and Mail

Frenchman Jean-Jacques Renouard de Villayer established a postal system in 1653. He set up mail boxes in Paris and delivered any letters which people posted in them, providing they used envelopes that he (and only he) sold. However, a jealous enemy put mice into the letterboxes. The mice chewed through the envelopes, destroying Renouard de Villayer's reputation and fledgling business in the process.

A timeline for the history of the American Post Office

The United States Post Office records these dates in its history.

1639   Richard Fairbanks' tavern in Boston, MA, was named as a repository for overseas mail.

1775   Benjamin Franklin was the first Postmaster General (under Continental Congress)

1823   Navigable waters were designated post routes by Congress.

1829   The 'Dead Letter Office' was opened.

1838   Railroads were designated post routes by Congress.

1845   Star routes were established.

1847   Postage stamps were introduced.

1855   Registered mail began.

1858   The introduction of street letterboxes

1860   The Pony Express started.

1863   Uniform postage rates, regardless of distance, are introduced and domestic mail is divided into three classes.

1885   Special delivery started.

1913   Parcel post began.

1918   Airmail began.

The first stamp

Rowland Hill (1795–1879) invented the modern adhesive postage stamp. The British 'Penny Black' stamp was issued on 6 May 1840. Hill wanted to reform the postal service so that the sender rather than the recipient was required to pay the postage. He also standardized postage so the same amount was paid wherever the letter was sent in the country.

Queen Victoria's portrait was engraved in profile on the stamp, setting the precedent for British stamps thereafter. Britain is the only country in the world that does not have its name on its stamps – but always has the head of its current reigning monarch.

The idea of prepaying for delivery of mail was so successful that other countries soon followed suit. Brazil adopted stamps in 1843, the USA in 1847 and France and Belgium in 1849. By 1860 around eighty-five countries issued stamps.

Stamp collecting

Stamp collecting began around the same time that stamps were first issued. Within twenty years, thousands of collectors and merchants catering to their needs sprung up across Europe in a phenomenon referred to as 'timbromania' (stamp madness). As the craze caught on, more and more businesses specializing in selling stamps appeared, the oldest of which is Stanley Gibbons, Ltd in London, founded in 1856.

Today it is thought that an estimated 200 million people collect stamps worldwide, and a network of shops, online trading sites, collectors' fairs, catalogue companies and clubs and associations exist to support the hobby.

The world's most expensive stamp

In 1855 in Sweden a printing error meant that a three-skilling stamp was printed on orange, rather than green, stock paper. When, in 1970, it was found to be genuine it became a rare collectible as the only 'Treskilling Yellow' in existence. Since its discovery in 1886 by a young collector the stamp has had various owners but it first achieved a million-dollar price tag when it was sold at auction in 1990. In May 2010 it made the headlines again when it was auctioned by David Feldman, a previous owner, in Geneva, Switzerland. The exact price remains undisclosed but it was revealed it went 'for at least the $2.3 million price it set a record for in 1996'.

The telegram

Telegrams consist of short messages transmitted by hand over a telegraph wire. The term 'telegram' emerged in the 1850s. Telegrams were especially popular in the 1920s and 30s, when it was cheaper to send a message than to place a telephone call. Since telegraph companies charged by the number of words in a message, a telegram style developed in which words were abbreviated and sentences clipped to remove unnecessary characters. The word 'stop' was used instead of the full stop since punctuation cost more that the four-character word.

In the UK, Ireland and the United States, telegram delivery boys were used to distribute messages, often on bicycles. In the UK, boys wore uniform and were required to complete a daily drill. Morning exercise was compulsory from 1915 to 1921.

By the 1960s, telegram usage had declined and the employment of telegram boys was no longer cost-effective. In 2006, Western Union delivered its final telegram, ending a 150-year service in the United States. In their long and often romanticized history, telegrams were used to announce the first flight, the start of World War I, and the fates of thousands of soldiers in wars that followed.

Notable telegrams

★   American author Mark Twain on hearing his obituary had been published sent a telegram from London in 1897: 'The reports of my death are greatly exaggerated'.

★   Sent from North Carolina in 1903, the following telegram announced a breakthrough moment by the Wright brothers in aviation history: 'Successfully four flights Thursday morning.'

★   In 1952, physicist Edward Teller sent the following to colleagues at Los Alamos about the first hydrogen bomb detonation: 'It's a boy'.

A Message from the Queen

Since 1917, the UK Sovereign has sent congratulatory messages to people in the Commonwealth celebrating notable birthdays and anniversaries. The message consists of a card contains a personalized missive, placed in a special envelope and delivered by the normal postal system.

The message originally came from the Private Secretary on behalf of the Sovereign. A message from 1919, sent to a centenarian on behalf of King George V in 1917 reads: 'His Majesty's hope that the blessings of good health and prosperity may attend you during the remainder of your days.'

The first messages were sent as telegrams by the Royal Mail's Inland Telegram Service. Messages were renamed Royal Court Telegram, probably in the early 1940s, and a Royal Crest was added to the top of the page. The telegram service was discontinued in 1982 and replaced by a telemessage, a combination of telegram and letter.

The Queen has sent approximately 110,000 telegrams and messages to centenarians in the UK and the Commonwealth while more than 520,000 telegrams and messages have been sent to couples celebrating their diamond wedding anniversary.

In 1997, the Queen sent messages of congratulations to those who were married in the same year as she, marking their golden wedding anniversaries. And in 2007 over 18,000 couples celebrating their diamond wedding anniversaries received congratulatory messages from the Queen and the Duke of Edinburgh.

Amusingly, the Queen Mother received an official 100th birthday greeting from her own daughter in 2000.

Who can read the post?

Generally letters and other documents cannot be read by anyone other than the intended recipient. In the US it is a violation of federal law for anyone other than the receiver to open mail. The privacy of correspondence is guaranteed by the Mexican Constitution and is also alluded to in the European Convention of Human Rights and the Universal Declaration of Human Rights. However, there are exceptions and in some cases, and in some countries, letters are opened and read. Military mail is often subject to censorship with incoming and outgoing post being read. The same applies to letters from and to prisoners.

The fountain pen

The quill pen had remained uncontested as the premier ink-writing mechanism for a thousand years until the late eighteenth century, when it began to face competition from a radical new design. Scribers began to search for a tool that would free them from constant inkwell-dipping. The oldest-known fountain pen was created in 1702 by Frenchman Nicholas Bion, but early designs were plagued by faults, including ink spills.

In 1884, a century later, insurance salesman Lewis Waterman was inspired to improve on these early designs when a leaky pen destroyed a sales contract. His patented device extracted ink from an internal reservoir, through to the nib, before depositing it on paper via gravity and capillary action. Ink writing had at last made the transition from being static to portable. Various developments to the ink reservoir design followed until Parker unveiled their capillary filling system in 1956.

By this time though, the fountain pen's market exclusivity was under threat by the invention of the ballpoint pen. But at the time ballpoints were relatively expensive and unreliable compared to the fountain pen, which by now had honed a combination of mass production and craftsmanship.

However, by the 1960s, the ballpoint pen – now developed to be low-cost and robust – had ensured its dominance in terms of casual usage. In the twenty-first century, the fountain pen appears to have retired from everyday use as a writing tool, inhabiting instead the realm of prestige. If you're looking to invest, the Aurora Diamante Fountain Pen, priced at $1.47 million, is the most expensive pen in the world and features 2,000 diamonds and a gold nib.

The fifty-year round robin letter

Women of the class of 1903 at Goucher College, Baltimore, Maryland wrote a 'round robin' letter to each other for almost fifty years, covering family life and also wider socio-political events, such as war, suffrage and the Depression. These excerpts are dated 1919.

> My dear Girls; It is years since I have used a typewriter but the suggestion that it would make the 'Robin' easier seems so sensible that I am going to try to write on this machine ... For two weeks after I left Baltimore I visited among the college friends in their homes and it certainly was a pleasure to be with them ... I came home to find my baby in the midst of a twelve weeks siege of 'whooping cough'. Along with it I had charge of the Child Welfare work in our town and now am interested in the returning soldiers ... (February, 1919)

Dear Classmates, Truly this robin is a gallant bird even tho he somehow skipped me in his flight three years ago and it has been seven long years since he alighted at my door, with his wonderful parcel of letters ... A little over two years ago, I heard the bells and horns and sirens, all over the city [Washington, DC] sound forth the news that Congress had declared war ... Soon we saw Washington change from a peaceful country town to a busy world center ... (July, 1919)

Dear Girls, Things have certainly been happening to us since we last wrote to each other, and while the war history of 1903 is just begun, it looks as if she were establishing her reputation as a leader in anything worthwhile that is going on. As I write, everyone is waiting expectantly and hopefully for our *** Senate to ratify the Peace Treaty. A general 'after the party' feeling seems to have seized everyone and especially those who were doing any kind of intensive work during the war. (October, 1919)

Long-awaited postcards

Sometimes correspondence takes a while to reach its destination. Some of the longest transit times occur with postcards.

★   A postcard from Exeter Cathedral, UK, arrived in Ipswich eighty-three years after it was sent. It was sent to a Miss Rix by someone called 'Babs' who had been to Ascot, on a train ride to Exeter and on to Dartmoor.

★   Vasilia Mazzotta from Connecticut, USA, received an Easter postcard from Greece, nearly forty-six years after it had been sent. The postcard was written by her grandfather, John B. Sitaras and addressed to Miss Vassoula Sitara (her maiden name), Hartford, Con. There was no street address, no ZIP code and no postage. It said, 'Dearest granddaughter, On the occasion of Holy day of Easter I send you this card to take an idea of Athens. I want you to enjoy Easter with all family. Kisses to Dad Mom & Johnny. I hug you. Bapou.'

★ A postcard turned up in a pizzeria in Fairfield, Ohio forty-nine years after it had been sent from Little Rock, Arkansas, USA. The card simply said: 'Arrived here this morning. Everything going fine. Donald.'

★ Another postcard was delivered seventy-nine years late. The card was sent in 1929 from Burnham-on-Crouch in the UK and was intended for Mr and Mrs Richardson of East Dulwich, London. It dropped through the letterbox of Arthur Davies and June Nicolopoulos nearly eight decades later.

Postmen in the movies

The following films feature postmen, postal systems and mail routes.

Il Postino (The Postman) (1994) – A shy postman strikes up a friendship with exiled Chilean poet Pablo Neruda and learns how to stand strong on life, love and politics.

The Postman (1997) – Kevin Costner plays a drifter who inadvertently ends up resuscitating US mail delivery in a dark post-apocalyptic world.

Pony Express Rider (1976) – Reasons to join the Pony Express in 1861? To find the man who killed your father in this case.

Frontier Pony Express (1939) - Set in the Civil War, Lassiter plans to send forged messages to troops on the west coast of California. He attempts to bribe Pony Express rider Roy Rogers, who must round up the villains and get the girl.

Pony Express (1953) – Western about the founding of mail routes into the West in the 1860s with historical figures such as Buffalo Bill and Wild Bill Hickok. Starring Charlton Heston.

PART TWO

Letterquette

Advice on writing: the basics

Over the centuries people have always sought to give advice on the best way to write the perfect letter. Even now there are numerous websites giving instructions. The following is a distillation of the current wisdom in the art of letter-writing – whether on paper or via email.

★ Write in a clear, conversational style. Keep it simple. Write to express, not to impress.

★ Present your best side – never write a letter, and particularly not an email, when angry. If you must, then put it aside and come back to it later or sleep on it – you may well choose not to send it at all. Remember that, once you hit Reply or drop the letter into the postbox, it is too late to retrieve.

★   Be consistent. Don't confuse the reader.

★   Use jargon sparingly, if at all. Avoid long words
    – they don't impress.

★   Break up your writing into short sections – long,
    unbroken blocks of text can intimidate or bore
    the reader. Start a new paragraph for each new
    thought. Read your letter aloud to check that
    sentences and paragraphs aren't too long.

★   Keep to the point. Check you've included all the
    relevant information.

The art of letter-writing

A good letter is a joy. A means of expressing ourselves, letters hold an important place in society, whether they are intended to inform, announce, persuade, declare or thank. A well-written letter is an art form and the ability to write well a powerful tool. Here are some literary opinions on letter-writing:

★ RAYMOND CHANDLER: 'By nature, a letter is a hybrid (part autobiography, part confessional, part report, part journal, part conversation), and a good letter tames the hybrid, even turning it into art. A good letter is an act of generosity: it uses the voice its writer thinks with, the voice he talks aloud to himself with.'

★ P. D. JAMES: 'No literary form is more revealing, more spontaneous or more individual than a letter.'

★ HÉLOISE: 'If a picture, which is but a mute representation of an object, can give such pleasure, what cannot letter inspire? They have souls, can speak, have in them all that force which expresses the transports of the heart.'

★ **HONORÉ DE BALZAC:** 'A letter is a soul, such a faithful copy of the beloved voice which speaks, that fragile souls count it among love's most precious treasures.'

★ **SAMUEL JOHNSON:** 'A man's letters are only the mirror of his heart. Whatever passes within him is there shown undisguised in its natural progress […] Is it not my soul laid open before you in these veracious pages? Do you not see me reduced to first principles? This is the pleasure of corresponding with a friend, where doubt and distrust have no place, and everything is said as it is thought.'

★ **SIR WALTER RALEIGH:** 'This is the triumph of letter-writing, that it keeps a more delicate image alive and presents us with a subtler likeness of the writer than we can find in the more formal achievements of authorship.'

Setting the tone

Whether you are writing a formal letter or a note to a friend, the way in which you set out your missive will set the tone. Formal letters will include job applications, resignations, letters of complaint, letters of request and most letters where you have not met or do not have an established relationship with the recipient.

How to set out a formal letter

If you are writing a formal letter, it is particularly important that you set it out correctly. An improperly set-out letter will create a bad impression from the off, and may affect the way in which your letter is received. You may have your own preferences, but the following advice will ensure your letter is acceptable in most formal circumstances. There are six main areas to focus on:

1. Your address
This should appear in the upper right-hand corer of the letter. Including your email address and phone number are optional, but do not put your name at the top of the address.

2. Recipient's address

This should be written in the upper left-hand corner of the letter but be set two or three lines below the first line of your own address. You may include the name of the recipient, their job title and their company name at the top of this address.

3. Date

This should appear on the right-hand side of the letter, at least one line lower than the last line of the recipient's address.

4. Salutation

If you know the name of the recipient, the salutation should be set out as 'Dear/Title/Name', e.g. Dear Mrs Jones. If you do not know the name of the person you are writing to, 'Dear Sir' or 'Dear Madam' is required, or even 'Dear Sir/Madam' when the gender is unknown. This should be placed on the left-hand side of the letter, a line or two below the date.

5. Closing

This should be placed below the body of the letter on the left-hand side. It signals the end of your correspondence and is therefore important in leaving a good final impression but it also links back to the salutation. If you have used a person's name in the salutation, the closing of the letter should be 'Yours sincerely'. If you have used 'Dear Sir' or 'Dear Madam', the closing should be 'Yours faithfully'.

6. Signature

In a formal letter, you should sign your name below the closing on the left-hand side of the page. Your name should then be printed beneath this.

Sample layout

> 28 Hazel Drive
> Little Holton
> Berkshire
> JU12 8KO
> UK

Mr C. Cook
Publicity Department
Bloomers Ltd
300 Broadway Avenue
WEST BEACH QLD 5021
AUSTRALIA

> 14 May 20XX

Dear Mr Cook,

Xxxxxxxxxxxxxxxxxxxxxxxxxxxxxxxxxxxxxxxxxxxxxxxxxxxx
xxxxxxxxxxxxxxxxxxxxxxxxxxxxxxxxxxxxxxxxxxxxxxxxxxxx
xxxxxxxxxxxxxxxxxxxxxxxxxxxxxxxxxxxxxxxxxxxxxxxxxxxx
xxx.

xxxxxxxxxxxxxxxxxxxxxxxxxxxxxxxxxxxxxxxxxxxxxxxxxxxx
xxxxxxxxxxxxxxxxxxxxxxxxxxxxxxxxxxxxxxxxxxxxxxxxxxxx
xxxxxxxxxxxxxxxxxxxxxxxxxxxxxxxxxxxxxxxxxxxxxxxxxxxx
xxx.

Yours sincerely,

Emma Wren

Alternative closings

For formal letters:

> Respectfully yours
>
> Yours respectfully
>
> Very truly yours
>
> Yours truly
>
> Kind regards

For less formal letters:

> As ever
>
> Ever yours
>
> Always yours

To a partner, good friend or family member:

> With love
>
> With all my love
>
> Affectionately
>
> Affectionately yours
>
> With much fondness

Evelyn Waugh chastizes his wife for being a poor letter-writer

7 January 1945

37 Military Mission [Dubrovnik]

Darling Laura, sweet whiskers, do try to write me better letters. Your last, dated 19 December received today, so eagerly expected, was a bitter disappointment. Do realize that a letter need not be a bald chronicle of events; I know you lead a dull life now, my heart bleeds for it, though I believe you could make it more interesting if you had the will. But that is no reason to make your letters as dull as your life. I simply am not interested in Bridget's children. Do grasp that. A letter should be a form of conversation; write as though you were talking to me. …

Do write & tell me what you are thinking & how you are looking. Be natural when you write. Don't send any more of these catalogues of family facts. Tell me what letters of mine you have had.

Evelyn.

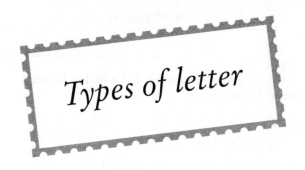

Types of letter

Letters between friends, family members or lovers are often used simply as a means of communicating news or sharing thoughts and intimacies. However, there are various types of letter – both formal and informal – that serve a more specific purpose, whether it be to advise, enquire, request or thank.

Thank-you letters

It has been said increasingly in recent years that letter-writing is a dying art. In our age of instant communication it is far easier to send a text or email than it is to put pen to paper. However, of all letter forms, the thank-you note has the most impact when it is written by hand. The very act of thanking demands an effort and thoughtfulness to ensure its sincerity. While many people do use email now, a handwritten note is still considered the most polite option.

Why say thank you?

The tradition of the thank-you note extends far back in human history, from the ancient Chinese and Egyptian cultures, who wrote on slips of papyrus, to fifteenth-century Europe, when the exchanging of handwritten notes became commonplace. While the handwritten letter may have gone out of fashion in recent years, that is not to say it has lost its impact. Gratitude is a virtue of good manners and we can all afford to extend a personal greeting in this increasingly impersonal world. It doesn't take long to thank someone but the effect is huge.

Thank you, personally

If you are sending a thank-you note to a friend or relative showing gratitude for a gift or their hospitality it is important to make it personal. For this reason, a handwritten, rather than an electronic, letter is a must. You might choose to use note cards or decorative stationery for your letter but most important is that you think before you write, to ensure that your thank-you letter does not read as if it were generated by a computer programme. Make sure you mention the gift or experience by name, commenting specifically on what you liked about it and stating why. For example, if you are given a framed picture of a place you have visited, you might comment on the happy memories it conjures, or on the perfect spot you have found for it on your wall. Laziness in writing a thank-you letter comes across as insincerity.

Thank you for a gift

[your address]

[date]

Dear

I am writing to thank you for the scarf. It was a lovely surprise and will certainly be very useful this winter.

I especially like the colour – how thoughtful of you to find one that matches my coat perfectly. I will be reminded of you when I am cosy and warm.

 I do hope you and the family are well and I look forward to seeing you in December.

Thank you again for your generosity.

With love,

Thank you, formally

There are many instances in which you may wish to thank an individual or organization with a more formal approach. As with all business letters, it is important that you stick to the accepted format, including the recipient's address, choosing an appropriate salutation and ending in the correct manner. The overall tone will depend a little on your relationship with the recipient – for example, if you are thanking a colleague or a charity – but, as with all thank-you letters, it is most important to be sincere and to reinforce your thanks with examples.

Princess Diana

Princess Diana was a prolific letter-writer who, despite her status and gruelling schedule, still understood the impact and importance of a handwritten thank-you note. She is said to have written her heartfelt thank-you letters in the evening while listening to classical music and always carried with her a set of royal thank-you notes so that she could express her gratitude promptly after an event.

Letters of condolence

Condolence letters are universally acknowledged as one of the hardest letters to write well, yet kind words at a time of sadness can offer much comfort to the recipient.

How to write a condolence letter

Letters of sympathy work best when their tone is affectionate without being gushing and the chosen words sound natural rather than forced. Think of a sympathy letter as a conversation you would have with the person, or family, only in letter form. Here is some advice:

★   Letters should be handwritten, usually relatively short (under a page) and sent promptly following the bereavement.

★   You can address them to the person in the family to whom you feel the closest or to the family as a whole.

★   Start by acknowledging the loss: 'I was sorry to hear of your recent bereavement'; 'I was terribly sad to hear of X's death', etc.

★ Express your sympathy. 'I want to express my heartfelt sympathy'; 'X was such a special person that no words are adequate.'

★ Include some detail on the deceased, his or her special qualities, to show your words are sincere.

★ Consider including a memory of how the deceased touched your life in some way.

★ Offer assistance – but don't offer help you cannot fulfil.

★ Including a well-chosen quote or poem is often considered good form – and shows you have spent time and care.

★ End with a thoughtful word or phrase such as 'My/Our thoughts are with you at this sad time.'

★ Sign off appropriately: 'With love and sympathy'; 'With my deepest sympathy', etc.

★ Put the letter away for a few hours before sending. Re-read it imagining how you would feel if you received it.

Example of a sympathy letter

[your address]

[date]

Dear Kate,

I was so sorry to hear about the death of John. I wanted to write and express my deepest sympathy as soon as I heard the news.

John was a kind and generous person, whose company I shall miss tremendously. I will never forget his help and advice when I first moved to London and was feeling homesick.

He was a brave man until the end and would often remark during our time together on how content he was in life.

If there is anything at all that I can help you with over the coming weeks please let me know, even if it is just picking the children up from school.

I am thinking of you and hope to see you soon.

Love,

George Eliot – the art of the sympathy letter
In this letter, dated 8 July 1870, the novelist writes to a close friend following the death of her uncle.

I did not like to write to you until Mr Lytton sent word that I might do so, because I had not the intimate knowledge that would have enabled me to measure your trouble; and one dreads of all things to speak or write a wrong or unseasonable word when words are the only signs of interest and sympathy that one has to give. I know now, from what your dear husband has told us, that your loss is very keenly felt by you, – that it has first made you acquainted with acute grief, and this makes me think of you very much. For learning to love any one is like an increase of property, – it increases care, and brings many new fears lest precious things should come to harm […]

Just under the pressure of grief, I do not believe there is any consolation. The word seems to me to be drapery for falsities. Sorrow must be sorrow, ill must be ill, till duty and love towards all who remain recover their rightful predominance. Your life is so full of those claims, that you will not have time for brooding over the unchangeable. Do not spend any of your valuable time now in writing to me, but be satisfied with sending me news of you through Mr Lytton when he has occasion to write to Mr Lewes […]

Letters of request

Whether you need a favour, assistance with a problem or help with your career, a letter is one of the most effective ways to get what you want. It offers you the chance to clearly state your request, without using superfluous words as you might do on the telephone, and to phrase your desires in as tactful, concise and elegant a manner as possible.

Tips on getting what you want

Whether your letter is to a stranger or to someone you know by name, here are some general pointers for getting the best response from your letters of request:

★   Keep the tone of your letter courteous and bright. You are far more likely to get a positive response if you yourself appear positive. For example, if you are requesting that a colleague change their irritating behaviour, try not to write the letter when you are feeling annoyed.

★   Make sure that what you want is set out very clearly. It may help to plan your letter, jotting down your main points before you begin writing.

★ If there are ways in which you could help your request be fulfilled, outline these too. For example, if you are asking for something to be sent to you, include a stamped addressed envelope.

★ Make sure you include your own contact details so that the recipient feels they can get in touch with any queries.

★ Thank the recipient for taking time to read your letter.

The Lady of the Manor asks for money

Margery Paston wrote in 1486 from the family estate in Norfolk to her husband, a lawyer, in London, asking for gold and catching up on everyday business and household matters. Her postscript is amusing.

To my master, John Paston, be this delivered

Right reverend and worshipful sir, in my most humble wise I recommend me to you, desiring to hear of your welfare, the which I beseech God to preserve to His pleasure and to your heart's desire. Sir, I thank you for the venison that ye sent me; and your ship is sailed out of haven as this day.

Sir, I send you by my brother William your stomacher of damask. As for your tippet of velvet, it is not here; Anne saith that ye put it in your casket at London.

Sir, your children be in good health, blessed be God.

Sir, I pray you send me the gold, that I spake to you of, by the next man that cometh to Norwich.

Sir, your mast that lay at Yarmouth is letten to a ship of Hull, 13s. and 4d., and if there fall any hurt thereto, ye shall have a new mast therefor.

No more to you at this time, but Almighty God have you in His keeping. Written at Caister Hall, the 21st day of January, in the first year of King Henry VII.

By your servant,

Margery Paston

I pray God no ladies no more overcome you, that you give no longer respite in your manners.

A strange request

Short-story writer Katherine Mansfield was married to John Middleton Murry, though the relationship was volatile. She was a most fervent writer of letters. This request, dated 24 March 1921, is unnerving in its politeness.

Dear Princess Bibesco,

I am afraid you must stop writing these little love letters to my husband while he and I live together. It is one of those things which is not done in our world.

You are very young. Won't you ask your husband to explain to you the impossibility of such a situation.

Please do not make me have to write to you again. I do not like scolding people and I simply hate having to teach them manners.

Yours sincerely,

Katherine Mansfield

You're fired! Letters of dismissal

Letters of dismissal are extremely difficult to phrase. Their aim is to release the recipient from employment without causing any conflict or evoking argument. Their tone must be formal – remember that anything you say in such a letter can be used in a court of law if for whatever reason the recipient challenges the dismissal. Here are some things to bear in mind:

★ Keep your words pleasant and soft – aim to preserve the self-respect of the recipient.

★ Remember that this is a legal document – write any letter in accordance with the policies of your company or organization.

★ Keep your statements simple. Explain exactly why the employment is being terminated.

★ Explain the procedures that have been followed and which need to be followed. If anything needs to be returned, make this clear.

★ Include full contact details in case the recipient needs to follow up the letter. Make it clear that support is offered if necessary.

★   Do not make the letter too long or involved – keep it professional, kind, yet succinct.

★   Show genuine concern; indicate that you're not happy writing the letter but are bound by policy.

★   Check the letter with someone knowledgeable in employment law.

Letters of resignation

A resignation letter needs to show tact and consideration, no matter what your feelings are for the work or the employer. Always remember that a reference may be required in the future.

Keep your letter brief, thanking your employer and offering a succinct reason for your resignation. Such reasons might be the offer of a new (more beneficial) position or the need to find a different challenge. If work cannot be cited as the reason for leaving, then a socially acceptable reason should be offered, such as poor health, family needs or relocation.

Example letter of resignation

[date]

Dear Mrs Lennox,

It is with great reluctance that I submit my resignation, effective 2 December, 2012.

My association with Sunshine Cereals has been enjoyable and I have learned much in my time with the business. However, I have been offered a position elsewhere which I cannot ignore, as it offers huge future potential and a chance to expand my skills.

Please accept my grateful thanks for the opportunities you have given me over the last five years. I have enjoyed working here and will retain very happy memories.

Yours sincerely,

Letters of complaint

If you feel very strongly about something, whether it is poor service or inconsiderate behaviour, writing a letter is one of the best ways to take action. It allows you the opportunity to state your point of view uninterrupted, and to choose the most effective tone.

Stand up for your rights

Before writing a letter of complaint, it is necessary to check your rights so that you can communicate clearly and convincingly. Here are some important points to consider:

★ If you are writing to a company or manufacturer, check consumer laws. These may vary in different countries so it is crucial that you know your entitlements.

★ If your complaint involves antisocial behaviour, for example, a noisy neighbour, consider seeking legal advice so that you are aware of how the law supports you.

★ Avoid threatening the recipient – you are far more likely to receive a favourable response if you keep your tone bright and concise.

★ Take time to find out the full name and title of the recipient. For example, if you are complaining to a local branch of a supermarket chain, find out the name of the store manager. This way your letter is more likely to reach your desired recipient quickly and to generate a more positive response.

★ Explain the problem concisely, detailing the cause and effect of your concern. Try to avoid sounding over-emotional, or including superfluous details.

Example letter of complaint

[address of recipient]

[date]

Dear Mr Plaza,

I am writing to complain about the discomfort caused to my family last weekend at one of your hotels.

We were very much looking forward to our break in Cornwall and had booked and paid for a sea-facing family room to take advantage of the views the hotel offers. However, on our arrival at the hotel on Friday night we were told that a mistake had been made, resulting from an error in the online booking facility, and that we would instead be provided with a room of lower quality to the one we had booked.

As it was late and we have two small children, we accepted this alteration with the promise that we would be moved in the morning and compensated for the inconvenience. However, the following day we were told a move would be impossible due to a plumbing problem in part of the hotel. We were not offered an apology, nor any compensation.

I am extremely unhappy about this situation. My wife and I were so looking forward to a rare break and our trip was overshadowed by the last-minute change and subsequent ill manners of your staff.

I am writing this letter not only to ask for compensation for receiving an inferior room to the one we had paid for, but also to say that, with regret, I may avoid booking any future trips with your hotel chain.

I look forward to receiving your response.

Yours sincerely,

Letter to the Editor

Sometimes abbreviated to LTTE or LTE, a letter to the editor is a letter sent to a publication, intended for publication. Most tend to comment on current issues or politics. They frequently respond to material that has been published in a previous issue (either praising or, more commonly, condemning). Others will respond to previous letters. Another common reason for LTEs is to correct a perceived error or misrepresentation.

Tips on writing Letters to the Editor

Countless letters are sent to publications every day, but if you want your message to stand out and maximize the chance of it being published, here are some tips to follow:

★ If you are responding to an article previously published, do so in good time. Your letter will not be printed if it refers to a commentary featured several weeks ago. Try to remain topical and create immediacy by responding directly to the target of the original piece and by doing so immediately.

★ Keep it brief: note the length of other LTEs and make sure you don't exceed the allotted word count. If you want your point to be heard, don't give editors the opportunity to cut your letter, nor to overlook it because it is too long for their publication.

★ Focus on one point, rather than several. Not only do you have limited space, but your letter will also have more resonance if you keep it simple. Make sure you back up your opinion with valid sources or facts and do not cloud your argument by meandering from your point.

★ Ensure both the publisher and readership will identify with your argument by aiming your letter at the correct literacy level. Too many long words and you may risk your letter being overlooked in place of one that is far more punchy.

Disgusted of Tunbridge Wells

A proverbial sign-off name in the United Kingdom for a letter to a newspaper complaining (usually in strident or excessive terms) about a subject that the writer feels is unacceptable or intolerable.

The term apparently dates back to the 1950s. Historian and former newspaper editor Frank Chapman attributes it to the staff of the former *Tunbridge Wells Advertiser*. The paper's editor, alarmed at a lack of letters from readers, insisted his staff write a few of their own to fill space. One signed his simply, 'Disgusted, Tunbridge Wells.'

The term was given a wide currency in the early 1950s by the BBC radio comedy series *Take It From Here*. However, recently some Tunbridge Wells residents have objected, calling it 'inappropriate' and 'stereotypical'.

Open letters

An open letter is generally considered to be a letter intended to be read by a wide audience. It normally takes the form of a letter addressed to an individual; however, once it is published (usually by means of a newspaper, magazine or on the Internet), it can be read by a much wider audience. The most common purpose of an open letter is to criticize someone's actions, but they may also be written to publicize one's own views, to prompt debate or for comedy value.

Letters patent are another form of open letter in which a legal document is mailed to an individual by the government yet also publicized so a wide audience is made aware of it.

J'Accuse

One of the most famous open letters in the world was penned by the French writer Emile Zola in 1898. It was intended for the President of France, Felix Faure, in defence of Captain Alfred Dreyfus, who stood accused of selling military secrets to the Germans.

Mr President,

Permit me, I beg you, in return for the gracious favour you once accorded me, to be concerned with regard to your just glory and to tell you that your record, so fair and fortunate thus far, is now threatened with the most shameful, the most ineffaceable blot.

What a clod of mud is flung upon your name – I was about to say your reign through this abominable Dreyfus affair. A court martial has but recently, by order, dared to acquit one Esterhazy - a supreme slap at all truth, all justice! And it is done; France has this brand upon her visage; history will relate that it was during your administration that such a social crime could be committed ...

Other famous open letters

Letters from a Farmer in Pennsylvania (1767–68) by lawyer John Dickinson, uniting colonists against the Townshend Acts

Martin Luther King's *Letter from Birmingham Jail* (1963)

Siegfried Sassoon's *A Soldier's Declaration*, questioning the judgement of Britain's leadership in World War I (1917)

William Banting's *Letter on Corpulence* (1863)

Albert Einstein's *Letter to an Arab* (1930)

Bobby Henderson's *Open Letter to the Kansas School Board* (2005)

David Cross's *Open Letter to Larry the Cable Guy* (2007)

Chain letters

A chain letter usually consists of a message that the recipient is asked to perpetuate by sending multiple copies to as many people as possible. The aim is to exponentially expand the readership of the original letter with each new recipient.

Chain letters originated as physical letters, sent in the post, but now tend to be passed on via email, text or through social networking sites. The letters often aim to manipulate the reader into not breaking the chain, threatening bad luck or even physical violence or death if you dare to ignore their message.

Here is a chain of facts about the sinister letterform:

★ The 'Prosperity Club' or 'Send-a-Dime' letter started in Denver, Colorado in 1935, swamping the Denver post office with hundreds of thousands of letters before spreading to other cities.

★ The 'Hawaiian Good Luck Totem' spread in thousands of forms, threatening people with bad luck if not forwarded.

★ The 'Mickey Mouse' email chain letter threatened death, injury, paranoia and bad luck if not forwarded to twenty-five people.

★ One chain letter on MSN Hotmail threatened to delete people's accounts if they didn't forward the message to all their contacts. It started 'Hey, it's Tara and John, the directors of MSN.'

★ Chain spiders ask people to sign a petition, adding their name to a long list of signatures, before passing it on.

★ The chain email of 'Carmen Winstead' (a girl who was pushed down a sewage drain) threatens: 'If you do not re-post/send this to ten people, Carmen will find you and kill you.'

★ Email chain letters often contains viruses and trojans.

★ In the US it is illegal to send chain letters involving pyramid schemes or the promise of money.

Poison pen letters

A poison pen letter is the term given to letters or notes usually sent anonymously which are unpleasant, abusive or malicious. The aim is to upset the recipient although, unlike blackmail, there is not usually any specific trade demanded.

★ The FBI has used poison pen letters as a tactic, targeting amongst others Martin Luther King Jr.

★ Fewer poison pen letters are sent now, presumably due to a decline in letter-writing generally. However in 2009 police investigated a series of letters sent to a family in North Yorkshire. One message read: 'It's a lovely day for a bonfire – yours …' There were also references to voodoo dolls. The public were asked if they could identify the handwriting.

★ On 13 August 1913 *The New York Times* referred to the 'now famous "poisoned pen" case' in which a Mrs Pollard sent unpleasant letters to her neighbour, Mrs Jones. Mrs Jones noticed that there was a defect in the letter 'e' in the missives, which had mostly been typewritten. Samples of type from Mrs Jones's typewriter were compared to the letters and indicated she was indeed the author.

Handwriting as evidence

The way in which we first learn to form letters, as well as the way in which we hold the writing implement and space our words is very difficult to change once it becomes habitual. The handwriting of every individual is unique and its analysis therefore forms an important forensic tool. Handwriting analysis is most often used to prove that two documents were written by the same person.

In the Lindbergh kidnapping of 1932 a ransom of $50,000 was paid but the twenty-month-old boy was never returned to his parents. His body was found a few miles from his home. After tracking the circulation of money used in the ransom payment, police located a suspect. Then forensics compared samples of his handwriting with that found on the ransom letter. A match was found, which strongly helped the case against the killer, who was convicted and executed in 1936.

Poison pen letters in literature and film

★ *Gaudy Night* by Dorothy Sayers. A Lord Peter Wimsey novel in which a poison pen messages join obscene graffiti and unsettling effigies to create a dark mood on campus at Shrewsbury College.

★ *The Girl Who Kicked the Hornet's Nest* by Stieg Larsson. In this third book in the Millennium trilogy, threatening letters are received from a sender who is nicknamed Poison Pen.

★ *Something Borrowed* by Paul Magrs. An investigation is started to find the sender of a poison pen letter.

★ *Le Corbeau* by Georges Clouzot. Anonymous poison pen letters are sent by someone signing themselves as Le Corbeau (the Raven) in this 1943 film. The term 'corbeau' entered the French language as a term used for the sender of anonymous letters.

* *Night at the Mocking Widow* by John Dickson Carr. A small English village is plagued by vicious poison pen letters sent by the 'Mocking Widow'.

* *The Mystery of the Spiteful Letters* by Enid Blyton. Children's book in which the Five Find-Outers have to discover the author of spiteful anonymous letters sent to several people in their village.

* *The Moving Finger* by Agatha Christie. A mystery concerning a brother and sister who become the victims of a poison pen letter.

Pen pals

Pen pals or penfriends are people who exchange news and thoughts by regularly writing to one another, in particular via postal mail (although modern penfriends also use email). In schools, schemes are often set up by teachers to help children practise foreign languages and learn about different lifestyles. Letters are usually written in the non-native language and many pen pals end up becoming good friends. Some continue to exchange letters for life.

For adults, there are pen pal clubs, often based around shared interests or hobbies. Many pen pals stick to postal mail as they can also include other material with their letters – it's common to add postcards, stamps, stickers, notecards and so on – anything light and flat enough to fit inside an envelope (known as a 'tuck-in').

Letter-writing as a form of therapy

Many psychotherapists believe that writing letters is a powerful form of self-therapy. Some research indicates that letters encourage the writer to open up, to focus their ideas and to reinforce their actions.

Often a person will be advised to write to someone who has hurt them, putting on paper exactly how they felt at the time and how they feel now, thus expressing all their unspoken feelings. Sometimes the therapist will advise burning the letter as a final way of letting go of the troublesome emotions.

Writing honestly can be a cathartic experience. Whatever your state of mind, age or position in life, letter-writing can bring clarity and a means of expressing emotions that have been repressed or forgotten.

A letter to my sixteen-year-old self

If you were to write a letter to your sixteen-year old self, what would it say? This was the premise behind a charity book, *Dear Me*, published in aid of the Elton John AIDS Foundation in 2009. Contributors ranged from rock stars to celebrity chefs and from actors to authors. Advice included:

★ 'Start moisturizing, particularly around the neck.' – SUE PERKINS

★ 'Take a bath or shower as often as possible.' – SIR RANULPH FIENNES

★ 'Try to avoid gossips and gossiping.' – JONATHAN ROSS

★ 'If anyone offers you Crystal Meth at a party make your excuses and leave.' – JULIAN CLARY

★ 'Stay away from drugs, they're a waste of time.' – SIR ELTON JOHN

★ 'Become a vegetarian.' – HAYLEY MILLS

★ 'Don't worry about diets.' – LYNDA LA PLANTE

★ 'Have fun. Sex is a good, not a bad thing.'
  – KEN RUSSELL

★ 'When he says he doesn't love you, believe him.
  He doesn't.' – EMMA THOMPSON

★ 'Go for it girl … keep dreaming.'
  – DEBBIE HARRY

The rise of the email

With the digital revolution sweeping its way through civilization it seemed inevitable that one of the first functions to be affected would be the handwritten letter. There are many advantages to emailing – the speed with which one can communicate, for example. Its immediacy – meaning that a message can travel from the sender to an inbox across the other side of the world in a matter of microseconds – puts the wait for letter deliveries in some quite substantial shade.

Emailing does, however, signify a loss of permanence or reference potential for future generations. The historians of tomorrow will be unable to analyse or document archives of personal emails in the same way as letters. Just as paper deteriorates and will fade, data sources can be lost for ever in the mire of a stuffed inbox or at the clutches of a computer virus.

Alongside socializing, emails have had the largest impact on the business world; changing the way in which companies send and receive information, and seemingly conjuring a whole new industry preoccupied with the constant refreshing of inboxes. With this shift, it is important to remember a few rules.

Netiquette: advice on emailing

'Netiquette' is the accepted standards for emailing in a business context. Advice includes:

* Avoid leaving the subject line blank

* Do not overuse CAPS or exclamation marks!!!!!!!

* Avoid using abbreviations for the sake of clarity – FYI, IMO, etc.

* Address the recipient appropriately and sign off with a similarly appropriate signature

* Misuse of the 'Reply to All' facility has resulted in numerous embarrassing security and personal issues, due to an email not being quite as shrouded in privacy as hoped. Check to whom you have addressed your email before you hit send.

PART THREE

What We Can Learn from Letters

Postcards from the past: a history lesson

'I regret that I am now to die in the belief that the useless sacrifice of themselves by the generation of 1776, to acquire self-government and happiness to their country, is to be thrown away by the unwise and unworthy passions of their sons, and that my only consolation is to be that I live not to weep over it.'

Thomas Jefferson to John Holmes, 22 April 1820

One of the main attractions of letters is their incredible variety. The telling of history is coloured by the personality of the letter-writer, and events from the past are inextricably woven with human emotion. And so, in tracing history through letter-writing, in reading these 'postcards from the past', we find pivotal moments are given an immediacy that could scarcely be captured by second-hand source material in a textbook.

Letters on science

On 7 January 1610 the Italian scientist Galileo Galilei wrote to politician Belisario Vinta, describing previously unknown details about the moon seen through his powerful telescope.

> ... the Moon is most evidently not at all of an even, smooth and regular surface, as a great many people believe of it and of the other heavenly bodies, but on the contrary it is rough and unequal ... I have observed many other details, and I hope to observe still more of them. We may believe that we have been the first in the world to discover anything of the celestial bodies from so near; and so distinctly.

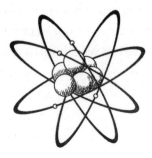

On 26 February 1867 Charles Darwin wrote to naturalist and explorer Alfred Russel Wallace. Wallace is best known for having proposed a theory of evolution that involved natural selection, prompting Darwin to develop his own.

> With respect to the beauty of male butterflies, I must as yet think that it is due to sexual selection … The reason of my being so much interested just at present about sexual selection is, that I have almost resolved to publish a little essay on the origin of Mankind, and I still strongly think (though I have failed to convince you, and this, to me, is the heaviest blow possible) that sexual selection has been the main agent in forming the races of man …

On 2 June1881 the French chemist Louis Pasteur wrote to his family, reporting his progress in creating a vaccine. He had been experimenting with anthrax vaccination at the farm of Pouilly-le-Fort near Melun.

> On Tuesday last […] we inoculated all the sheep, vaccinated and non-vaccinated, with very virulent splenic fever. It is not forty-eight hours ago. Well, the telegram tells me that, when we arrive at two o'clock this afternoon, all the non-vaccinated subjects will be dead … as to the vaccinated ones, they are all well; the telegram ends by the words: 'stunning success' […] Joy reigns in the laboratory and in the house. Rejoice dear children.

*

In 1911, Henri Poincaré and Marie Curie wrote to the Federal Institute of Technology at Zurich, recommending a young man called Albert Einstein:

> […] Herr Einstein is one of the most original minds that we have ever met. In spite of his youth he already occupies a very honourable position amongst the foremost savants of his time […] The future will give more and more proofs of the merits of Herr Einstein, and the University that

succeeds in attaching him to itself may be certain that it will derive honour from its connection with the young master.

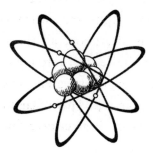

An early warning

Kuyuk Khan was the grandson of Genghis Khan, supreme ruler of the Mongol empire from 1246 to 1248. It is recorded that he was an arrogant, harsh and vindictive ruler. These traits certainly shine through in these excerpts from a letter written to Pope Innocent IV.

> By the power of the Eternal Heaven, we are the all-embracing Khan of all the great nations. It is our command: This is a decree, sent to the great Pope that he may know and pay heed [...]

> [...] you have sent us an offer of subordination, which we have accepted from the hands of your envoy. You have said it would be well for us to become Christians. You write to me in person about this matter and have addressed a request to me. This we cannot understand [...]

> You in person, at the head of the monarchs, all of you, without exception, must come to tender us service and pay us homage, then only will we recognize your submission. But if you do not obey the commands of Heaven and run counter to our orders, we shall know that you are our foe.

That is what we have to tell you. If you fail to act in accordance with this, how can we foresee what will happen to you? Heaven alone knows.

Epistolae – medieval women's letters

Professor Joan Ferrante of Columbia University has collected and translated (from the Latin) a collection of letters to and from women in the Middle Ages, from the fourth to the thirteenth centuries. The following is part of a twelfth-century letter sent from Hildegard of Bingen to Elisabeth of Schoenau.

I, a poor little form and earthen vessel, speak these things not from myself but from the serene light: Man is a vessel which God fashioned for himself, which he imbued with his spirit, so that he might accomplish his works in him; for God does not work as man does but by the order of his command all things are carried out. Grasses, brush, and trees appeared; the sun, the moon, and the stars also came about by his care, and the waters produced fish and birds, and flocks and beasts arose as well, which minister all things to men, as God commanded […]

... O daughter, let God make you a mirror of life. But I too lie in the pusillanimity of my mind, fatigued much by fear, sounding a little, at times, like the small sound of a trumpet from the living light. Whence God help me that I may remain in his ministry.

On the virtues of women

Christine de Pisan, the fourteenth-century author of *City of Ladies* (an imagined city without men), wrote this open letter to women as an introduction to the book.

> And you, virgin maidens, be pure, simple, and serene, without vagueness, for the snares of evil men are set for you. Keep your eyes lowered, with few words in your mouths, and act respectfully. Be armed with the strength of virtue against the tricks of the deceptive and avoid their company.

> And widows, may there be integrity in your dress, conduct and speech; piety in your deeds and way of life; prudence in your bearing; patience (so necessary!), strength, and resistance in tribulations

and difficult affairs; humility in your heart, countenance, and speech; and charity in your works.

In brief, all women – whether noble, bourgeois, or lower-class – be well-informed in all things and cautious in defending your honour and chastity against your enemies! My ladies, see how these men accuse you of so many vices in everything. Make liars of them all by showing forth your virtue, and prove their attacks false by acting well …

Rallying Reims

When Joan of Arc wrote this letter on 16 March 1430, she had under a year to live (and had been told this by her inner voices). The letter was written to the people of Reims to encourage and reassure them as the town was under threat of attack.

Dearly beloved friends, how I long to see you. I, Joan the Maid, have received your letters in which you tell of your fear that you will soon be under siege. I want you to know that this fate will not befall you, if only I can meet with the enemy first. And if I cannot manage to get there in time and they do come, close your gates and rest assured that I will come very shortly. If I find them besieging you, I'll force them to take to their spurs so quickly that they won't know whether they are coming or going and I'll raise the siege, if there is one, straight away. I will write no more for the present, as I know that you are good and loyal people. I pray to God to protect you. Written at Sully the 16th day of March. I would tell you some news that would cheer you, but I fear that the letter may fall into enemy hands and that they would discover the news, and not you.

Letters of Note

Letters of Note (www.lettersofnote.com) is a blog that attempts 'to gather and sort fascinating letters, postcards, telegrams, faxes and memos'. Contributors send in scanned copies and photos of interesting correspondence. The letters include those from famous people, such as a touching (if typically foul-mouthed) note from Iggy Pop and an enthusiastic letter to an early fan from David Bowie, an excerpt of which follows:

> In answer to your questions, my real name is David Jones and I don't have to tell you why I changed it. 'Nobody's going to make a monkey out of you,' said my manager. My birthday is January 8th and I guess I'm 5'10". There is a Fan Club here in England, but if things go well in the States then we'll have one there I suppose. It's a little early to even think about it.

Napoleon and the King

Not all of Napoleon's letters were as sweet as those he sent to Josephine. Yet he was not a mean-natured correspondent. The letters he and Louis XVIII exchanged show a grudging admiration between the two men.

From Louis to Napoleon:

> You are taking a long time to give me back my throne: there is a danger you may miss the opportunity. Without me you cannot make France happy, while without you I can do nothing for France. So be quick and let me know what positions and dignities will satisfy you and your friends.

From Napoleon to Louis:

> I have received your letter. I thank you for your kind remarks about myself. You must give up any hope of returning to France: you would have to pass over 100,000 dead bodies. Sacrifice your private interests to the peace and happiness of France. History will not forget. I am not untouched by the misfortunes of your family. I will gladly do what I can to render your retirement pleasant and undisturbed. Bonaparte.

Great Plague of London

In a letter to Lady Elizabeth Carteret, dated 4 September 1665, Samuel Pepys presents a harrowing picture of a city on its knees.

> […] I having stayed in the city till above 7,400 died in one week of them above 6,000 of the plague, and little noise heard day nor night but tolling of bells; till I could walk Lumber Street and not meet twenty person from one end to the other, and not fifty upon The Exchange; till whole families (ten and twelve together) have been swept away; till my very physician, Dr. Burnet, who undertook to secure me against any infection (having survived the month of his own being shut up) died himself of the plague; till the nights (though much lengthened) are grown too short to conceal the burials of those that died the day before, people being thereby constrained to borrow daylight for that service; lastly, till I could find neither meat nor drink safe, the butcheries being everywhere visited, my brewer's house shut up, and my baker with his whole family dead of the plague […]

The letter that started the diet industry

William Banting was an undertaker and coffin maker. In 1863, he wrote a booklet called *Letter on Corpulence, Addressed to the Public*, which outlined his personal diet plan in the form of an open letter testimonial.

Banting had tried all kinds of fasts and exercise regimes before being given a diet plan by a doctor. The diet consisted of four meals per day, based around meat, green vegetables, fruit and dry wine. He avoided sugar, starch, beer, milk and butter. In short, it was the first low-carbohydrate diet. It worked – and he proceeded to tell the world of his success.

Banting published his letter at his own expense. It became hugely popular – people would ask 'Do you Bant?' referring initially to his method and *banting* became synonymous with dieting. The third and subsequent editions were published by Harrison, London. Banting's booklet remains in print today.

Injustice anywhere

Martin Luther King, Jr. was jailed in Birmingham, Alabama, after a non-violent protest against segregation in 1963. The open letter he wrote whilst there – 'Letter from Birmingham Jail' (16 April 1963) was printed in *The Christian Century* and *The Atlantic Monthly* and became one of the most famous open letters ever written. Here is an excerpt:

> … I am in Birmingham because injustice is here … . I cannot sit idly by in Atlanta and not be concerned about what happens in Birmingham. Injustice anywhere is a threat to justice everywhere. We are caught in an inescapable network of mutuality, tied in a single garment of destiny. Whatever affects one directly, affects all indirectly. Never again can we afford to live with the narrow, provincial 'outside agitator' idea. Anyone who lives inside the United States can never be considered an outsider anywhere within its bounds …

Pivotal moments

Here is a collection of excerpts from letters written at pivotal moments in world history, though the writers may scarcely have known it at the time:

★ Saint Jerome wrote to Eustochrium in 412 BC to tell of the fall of Rome to the 'barbarians': 'Who would believe that Rome, built up by the conquest of the whole world, had collapsed, that the mother of nations had become also their tomb ... .'

★ Pliny the Younger wrote to the Emperor Trajan in AD 112 about the rise of a religious cult called Christianity. 'I have never been present at an examination of Christians. Consequently I do not know the nature or the extent of the punishments usually meted out to them ... I have therefore postponed any further examinations and hastened to consult you. It is not only the towns, but villages and rural districts too which are infected through contact with this wretched cult.'

★ Conquistador Hernando Pizarro described the capture of the Inca King in 1533: 'In the space of two hours ... all these troops were annihilated. That day, six or seven thousand Indians lay dead on the plain and many more had their arms cut off ... Atahualpa himself admitted that we had killed seven thousand of his Indians in that battle. It was an extraordinary thing to see so great a ruler captured in so short a time, when he had come with such might.'

★ Catherine the Great wrote to Count Poniatowski in 1762 detailing the plot that made her Empress of Russia: 'I am sending Count Keyserling at once to Poland to make you King after the death of the present King ... My accession to the throne had been under preparation for six months. Peter III had lost still more of the little understanding that he once possessed. He tried to thrust his head through the wall ... I must observe a thousand proprieties and take a thousand things into consideration; and withal I feel the whole burden of the business of government ... Adieu! There are some very strange lots in the world.'

★ Neville Chamberlain wrote to Adolf Hitler in September 1938, during the Sudetenland crisis: 'The Czech Government cannot, of course, withdraw their forces, so long as they are faced with the prospect of forcible invasion; but I would urge them to withdraw from the areas where the Sudeten Germans are in a position to maintain order.'

Dear John: letters in wartime

… this appalling Horror (we are steeped up to our necks in blood) … .These poor fellows bear pain and mutilation with an unshrinking heroism which is really superhuman, and die, or are cut up without a complaint.

Florence Nightingale to Sir William Bowman in 1854, during the Crimean War

If we had to rely on formal written accounts of wartime, our knowledge would be very narrow – limited to stiff reports from the rich, powerful and educated. Letters, however, often show us that we have more in common with our distant forebears than we might imagine. In this section, we look at letters written during, or on the theme of, war. Often they reveal the personal conflicts fought amid those between nations, and broaden our understanding of what it was to live through the horrors of war.

Edith Cavell's last letter

Nurse Edith Cavell was running a clinic in Brussels in August 1914 when Germany invaded Belgium. Later that year she began aiding British (and some French and Belgian) soldiers to escape what had become occupied Belgium. The Germans arrested her in August 1915 and charged her with harbouring enemy (i.e. Allied) soldiers. After more than two months in prison (the last two weeks in solitary confinement), she was tried by court martial and sentenced to death. The British government was powerless to assist her; she was shot by firing squad in the Belgian national shooting range, Brussels, at 6 a.m. on 12 October 1915. The night before her death her thoughts were full of concern for her young friend, to whom she wrote the following letter.

> My Dear Girl, how shall I write you this last day? Standing where I stand now, the world looks far away already. I worried about you a great deal at first, but I know that God will do for you abundantly above all that I can think or ask, and He loves you so much better than I. I do earnestly beseech you to try and live as I would have you live. Nothing matters when one comes to this last hour but a clear conscience before God, and life looks so wasted and full of wrong-doing and things left undone.

You have helped me often, my dear, and in ways you little dreamed of, and I have remembered our happy holidays with mother and many small pleasures. I want you to go to England at once now, and ask to put you where you can be cured. Don't mind how hard it is; do it for my sake. And then try to find something useful to do – something to make you forget yourself while making others happy . . .

Forgive me if I have been severe sometimes; it has been a great grief to me to remember it. I think I was too anxious about you last year, and that is why. I am sure you will forget it now, and only remember that I love you, and love you still.

An open letter to a Nazi

In March 1933, the novelist, poet and philosopher Lion Feuchtwanger had his house confiscated by the Nazis. They destroyed his library and his writings. His house was given to a member of the National Socialist Party. When he received the news, Feuchtwanger addressed this letter to the new occupant of his house.

Dear Sir: I do not know your name or how you came into possession of my house. I only know that two years ago the police of the Third Reich seized all my property, personal and real, and handed it over to the stock company formed by the Reich for the confiscation of the properties of political adversaries ...

How do you like my house, Herr X? Do you find it pleasant to live in? Did the silver-grey carpets in the upper rooms come to grief while the S.A. men were looting?

... I wonder to what use you have put the two rooms which formerly contained my library? I have been told, Herr X, that books are not very popular in the Reich in which you live, and whoever shows interest in them is likely to get into difficulties. I, for instance, read your Führer's book and guilelessly remarked that his 140,000 words were 140,000 offenses against the spirit of the German language. The result of this remark is that you are now living in my house ...

Doesn't it sometimes seem odd to you that you should be living in my house? Your Führer is not generally considered a friend of Jewish literature.

Isn't it, therefore, astounding that he should have such a strong predilection for the Old Testament? I myself have heard him quote with much fervour, 'An eye for an eye, a tooth for a tooth' (by which he may have meant, 'A confiscation of property for literary criticism'). And now, through you, he has fulfilled a prophecy of the Old Testament – the saying, 'Thou shalt dwell in houses thou hast not builded.'

… With many good wishes for our house,

Lion Feuchtwanger

Will nothing be done?

Emily Hobhouse, a British welfare campaigner, criticized the British concentration camps during the Boer War in an open letter to the Secretary of State for War in 1903. It was sent to the press: 'Will nothing be done? Will no prompt measures be taken to deal with this terrible evil?'

Dear John . . .

The phrase 'Dear John letter' has come to mean a letter ending a relationship. According to the *Oxford English Dictionary* the term probably originated during World War II and referred to letters from wives and sweethearts announcing the relationship was over. References from the *OED* include, in date order:

★ 1945: '"Dear John," the letter began. "I have found someone else whom I think the world of. I think the only way out is for us to get a divorce." They usually began like that, those letters that told of infidelity on the part of the wives of servicemen … The men called them "Dear Johns".'

★ 1947: 'It was a "Dear John". Quite a lot of the fellows had already had their "Dear Johns".'

★ 1957: 'There was a note from Fenny on the kitchen table. For the moment he enjoyed the irony of thinking it might be what the Americans called a "dearjohn".'

★ 1964: 'Peter … had gone to war … in love with a girl named Elizabeth Schofield … He had received a "Dear John" letter from Elizabeth, telling him she was married.'

POWs lose love

'Dear John' letters, informing a POW of his wife or fiancée's unfaithfulness, were the most dreaded in World War II prisoner-of-war camps. In most camps such letters were pinned up on the camp notice board for all the inmates to see – not to be cruel, but so a rough and ready form of group therapy could follow. Some of the letters are quite staggering in their honesty:

★ 'Sorry. Married your father. Mother.'

★ 'I'm so glad you were shot down, before flying became dangerous.'

★ 'Our engagement has ended, as I'd rather marry a '44 hero than a '43 coward.'

★ I am filing for divorce. Mother and I have discussed it since it is four years since you went down and we decided it was best.'

★ 'Don't bother to hurry home as I am living with an American and having a lovely time. I am having his baby soon but forgive me as mother has done. Ted is sending you cigarette parcels.'

Letter to Vietnam

During the conflict in Vietnam, photographer Steven Curtis (www.stevencurtis.com) worked on assignments on his two tours of duty with the Marine Corps. When not working, he endeavoured to capture the human side of war. He remembers the effects of 'Dear John' letters on his comrades.

Almost as feared as the enemy bullet was the 'Dear John' letter. Hardly a week went by without someone getting one. Mail call was often referred to as the 'Dear John' roundup. They were almost always the same story. A guy would get a letter from his girl informing him that she didn't want to hurt him but she'd met someone else and, from now on, she just wanted to be friends. Since they hadn't seen each other in seven or eight months, how could he expect her to be faithful for an entire year? After coming to terms with the one I got, I began to counsel others who got them by telling them to look at it as a blessing in disguise. Any woman who didn't have the strength of character to stand by her man in his time of need wasn't worth going back to anyway.

I always wondered if the people back home who wrote letters such as these had any idea of how psychologically devastating they were. We had so few personal possessions of a sentimental nature. Letters from a loved one were never thrown out but read and re-read – sometimes to our closest buddy, but mostly to ourselves in moments of solitude. I don't ever remember seeing a guy take out a Bible to read, but I do remember a lot of guys re-reading their love letter as if it were the Bible. I guess we all felt as if God had forsaken us but, please, Lord, don't let our women forsake us too.

A letter of warning

President Franklin Roosevelt received a letter from Albert Einstein in 1939, four weeks before Hitler invaded Poland. The letter advised that the US should start research into nuclear weapons and complete the bomb before the Germans did. At this time most American physicists doubted that atomic energy or atomic bombs were a possibility. The letter was actually mainly the work of Leo Szilard, a Hungarian-born scientist working in the US. He sent two letters to Einstein who, in turn, signed them and returned them, telling Szilard to use whichever he thought the most effective. Here is an excerpt from the one that reached Roosevelt.

In the course of the last four months it has been made probable that it may become possible to set up a nuclear chain reaction in a large mass of uranium, by which vast amounts of power and large quantities of new radium-like elements would be generated. Now it appears almost certain that this could be achieved in the near future. This new phenomenon would also lead to the construction of bombs, and it is conceivable – though much less certain – that extremely powerful bombs of a new type may thus be constructed. A single bomb of this type, carried by boat or exploded in a port, might very well destroy the whole port together with some of the surrounding territory …

Einstein later regretted the letters. In November 1954, less than a year before his death, he told the physicist Linus Pauling: 'I made one great mistake in my life – when I signed the letter to President Roosevelt recommending that atom bombs be made. But there was some justification – the danger that the Germans would make them.'

The Blitz

Stanley Lupino, an actor and Air Raid Precaution warden in London during the Blitz, wrote to his wife in the US on 13 October 1940. 'The intensified gun barrage we are putting up is so terrific all the birds in the trees are fallen dead in thousands. It is unceasing, the sky aflame with shells bursting like thousands of red hot stars and shrapnel falling like rain ...'

Edith Wharton writes to Henry James from the Front during the First World War

During World War I, American novelist Edith Wharton wrote to her close friend, the novelist Henry James, from Verdun in France. The following extracts show her skill in conjuring the chaos and clamour of wartime for her reader.

> ... The Germans were firing from the top at the French trenches below (hidden from us by an intervening rise of the ground): & the French were assaulting, & their puffs & flashes were halfway

up the hill. And so we saw the reason why there are to be so many wounded at Clermont tonight!

Picture this all under a white winter sky, driving great flurries of snow across the mud-and-cinder-coloured landscape, with the steel-cold Meuse winding between beaten poplars – Cook standing with Her in a knot of mud-coated military motors & artillery horses, soldiers coming & going, cavalrymen riding up with messages, poor bandaged creatures in rag-bag clothes leaning in doorways, & always, over & above us, the boom, boom, boom of the guns on the grey heights to the east.

Her letters prompted James to respond: 'Your whole record is sublime, and the interest and the beauty and the terror of it all have again and again called me back to it ...'

Finished with the war: a soldier's declaration

In 1917, the poet Siegfried Sassoon wrote this statement letter (with the assistance of Bertrand Russell and John Middleton Murry) to his commanding officer, refusing to return to duty. Copies of the letter were distributed to influential people and the press; it was published by the *Bradford Pioneer* on 27 July and read to the House of Commons three days later.

> I am making this statement as an act of wilful defiance of military authority because I believe that the war is being deliberately prolonged by those who have the power to end it. I am a soldier, convinced that I am acting on behalf of soldiers. I believe that the war upon which I entered as a war of defence and liberation has now become a war of aggression and conquest. I believe that the purposes for which I and my fellow soldiers entered upon this war should have been so clearly stated as to have made it impossible to change them and that had this been done the objects which *actuated* us would now be attainable by negotiation.

I have seen and endured the sufferings of the troops and I can no longer be a party to prolonging these sufferings for ends which I believe to be evil and unjust. I am not protesting against the conduct of the war, but against the political errors and insincerities for which the fighting men are being sacrificed.

On behalf of those who are suffering now, I make this protest against the deception which is being practised upon them; also I believe it may help to destroy the callous complacency with which the majority of those at home regard the continuance of agonies which they do not share and which they have not enough imagination to realize.

The letter was viewed by many as treasonous but, rather than arrest Sassoon, the Under-Secretary of State for War instead sent him to Craiglockhart War Hospital, where he was treated for shellshock.

Eternal love

Company Sergeant-Major James Milne struggled to write to his wife during World War I.

> My own Beloved Wife, I do not know how to start this letter or not. The circumstances are different from any other which I ever wrote before. I am not to post it but will leave it in my pocket and if anything happens to me someone will perhaps post it. We are going over the top this forenoon and only God in Heaven knows who will come out of it alive ... Eternal love from
>
> Yours for Ever and Ever Jim

He survived the war.

Affairs of the heart: love letters

… the first glance to see how many pages there are, the second to see how it ends, the breathless first reading, the slow lingering over each phrase and each word, the taking possession, the absorbing of them, one by one, and finally the choosing of the one that will be carried in one's thoughts all day, making an exquisite accompaniment to the dull prose of life.

Edith Wharton, on receiving a love letter

Whether long or short the love letter allows the writer the opportunity to express feelings in solitude and to give shape to his or her emotions.

Historically, love letters may have been written in a poetic form – a sonnet, for example. Today, they may be constructed over email. Yet, by their very nature, love letters are personal and ring most true when delivered by post or in person, rather than electronically.

As well as representing tokens of devotion, love letters also hold a symbolic value, bound up in the strength of the relationship between writer and recipient. When love is lost, letters are often burned to represent the breaking of a bond.

Billet-doux

A now archaic term for a love letter, from the French *billet*, meaning 'short note' and *doux*, meaning 'sweet'.

A lost art?

Until the twentieth century, love letters were essential in progressing romantic relationships. Passionate sentiments were captured on paper and delivered to the recipient as a physical and lasting declaration. Imagine the excitement of receiving a letter from an absent love when the post was your only means of communicating. Once, a love letter would have sent a heart fluttering.

Fewer and fewer people take the trouble to write by hand nowadays, and the bond between sender and recipient has been replaced by the looseness of instant communication. But the immutability of the physical letter cannot be eroded – anyone who has ever received a love letter will treasure it. If you want to make an enduring declaration, the letter has no rival.

Lessons in love: advice on writing

Every love letter is different because it's personal to both the sender and recipient. But while love may have no bounds, there are some straightforward tips to follow if you want to get the most out of your writing.

★   Date your letter. Remember that it will be a keepsake and may be re-read in years to come.

★ Open with a sincere and heartfelt salutation. Don't shy away from using pet names if they mean something, or flattery if it sets the right tone.

★ Explain how you feel about your loved one. You might like to imagine the time when you were last together and the emotions you felt. Try to describe these honestly and confidently. Love cannot be too bold.

★ Convey what you love about the recipient – was it a specific character trait, a look or an action? Write why they are special and what it means to be with them.

★ Take time to get it right. Draft your letter several times over and ensure that your final version is carefully presented just how you wish it to be.

★ End by considering the past, the present and the future. How has this person changed your life and how do they continue to do so?

★ Close with a meaningful phrase or a heartfelt goodbye. Just writing 'From David' would be going out with a whimper, when you really want the recipient's heart to pound. Words such as 'All my love, always' may not be unique but they are simple and expressive.

The oldest Valentine

Uncovered by the British Library, the oldest-known Valentine's Day message is thought to date back to 1477 and was written in Norfolk. The message is from Margery Brews to her fiancé John Paston and concerns their forthcoming nuptials. It begins: 'Right reverent and worshipful and my right well-beloved valentine, I recommend me unto you full heartedly, desiring to hear of your welfare, which I beseech Almighty God long for to preserve unto his pleasure and your hearts desire.' Margery goes on to explain that she has asked her mother to beseech her father to increase her dowry, but maintains that if John loves her he ought to marry her regardless of money: 'But if you love me, as I trust verily that you do, you will not leave me therefore.'

Openings to love letters

A love letter rarely requires formality and you may turn to the most fanciful of salutations with which to open your missive. Using your love's first name or other term of endearment sets the tone for the personal declarations to follow.

Here are some example openings of real-life love letters:

★ 'Unspeakably belovedest'
(Nathaniel Hawthorne to Sophia Peabody)

★ 'My Own Dearest Wifie'
(Charles Stewart Parnell to Kitty O'Shea)

★ 'My angel, my all, my very self'
(Beethoven to unknown)

★ 'Alpha and Omega'
(Horatio Nelson to Emma Hamilton)

★ 'Chère amie, chères delices'
(Marcel Proust to Laure Hayman)

★ 'To ye most loving wife alive'
(Chidiock Tichborne to Agnes Tichborne)

* ★ 'My Very Precious One'
  (Czarina Alexandra to Czar Nicholas II)

* ★ 'My ever-new Delight'
  (John Hervey, First Earl of Bristol, to Elizabeth Hervey)

* ★ 'Wonderful Boy'
  (Sarah Bernhardt to Victorien Sardou)

Love letters from history

We can learn a great deal about past events from the correspondence of the time. But preserved love letters often reveal to us the human hearts behind historical figures.

Abelard and Héloise

Peter Abelard (1079–1142) was a French philosopher. Héloise (1101–64) was the niece of Canon Fulbert. They are one of the most celebrated couples; renowned for their passionate love affair, their correspondence, and the tragedy that parted them. Unable to live openly as man and wife, they went into separate religious establishments and it was from here that they wrote their famous correspondence in Latin, mainly concerning lost love.

From Abelard to Héloise:

> Write no more to me, Héloise, write no more to me; 'tis time to end communications which make our penances of nought avail. We retired from the world to purify ourselves, and, by a conduct directly contrary to Christian morality, we became odious to Jesus Christ. Let us no more deceive ourselves with remembrance of our past pleasures; we but make our lives troubled and spoil the sweets of solitude. Let us make good use of our austerities and no longer preserve the memories of our crimes amongst the severities of penance. Let a mortification of body and mind, a strict fasting, continual solitude, profound and holy

meditations, and a sincere love of God succeed our former irregularities.

From Héloise to Abelard:

I read the letter I received from you with great impatience: in spite of all my misfortunes I hoped to find nothing in it besides arguments of comfort. But how ingenious are lovers in tormenting themselves. Judge of the exquisite sensibility and force of my love by that which causes the grief of my soul. I was disturbed at the superscription of your letter; why did you place the name of Héloise before that of Abelard? What means this cruel and unjust distinction? It was your name only – the name of a father and a husband – which my eager eyes sought for. I did not look for my own, which I would if possible forget, for it is the cause of all your misfortunes. The rules of decorum, and your position as master and director over me, opposed that ceremony in addressing me; and love commanded you to banish it: alas! You know all this but too well!

My dear Lord

Early English aristocratic matches were usually made for political reasons and devoid of love, so this letter from Lady Pelham to Sir John Pelham, written in 1399, is unusual in its fondness. It is one of the earliest love letters extant in the English language.

My dear Lord,

I recommend me to your high lordship, with heart and body and all my poor might. And with all this I thank you as my dear Lord, dearest and best beloved of all earthly lords. I say for me, and thank you, dear Lord, with all this that I said before for your comfortable letter that you sent me from Pontefract, that came to me on Mary Magdalene's day; for by my troth I was never so glad as when I heard by your letter ye were strong enough with the Grace of God to keep you from the malice of your enemies […]

From Henry VIII to Anne Boleyn

Perhaps most renowned for his six marriages, Henry VIII's rule was also characterized by the separation of the Church of England from Rome. Henry sought an annulment from his first marriage to Catherine of Aragon in order to marry his sweetheart and infatuation, Anne Boleyn.

A series of undated love letters written to Anne were found in the Vatican Library. Her replies have been lost. The following is one of Henry's letters.

> Myne awne Sweetheart, this shall be to advertise you of the great ellingness [loneliness] that I find her since your departing, for I ensure you, me thinketh the Tyme longer since your departing now last than I was wont to do a whole Fortnight; I think your Kindness and my Fervence of Love causeth it, for otherwise I wolde not thought it possible, that for so little a while it should have grieved me, but now that I am comeing toward you, me thinketh my Pains by half released, and also I am right well comforted, insomuch that my Book maketh substantially for my Matter, in writing whereof I have spent above IIII Hours this Day, which caused me now write the shorter Letter to you at this Tyme, because of some Payne

in my Head, wishing my self (specially an Evening) in my Sweethearts Armes, whole pretty Duckys [breasts] I trust shortly to kysse. Writne with the Hand of him that was, is, and shall be yours by his will, H.R.

Napoleon in love

Napoleon is well known for his passionate love for his wife Josephine although he also wrote to other lovers, including Marie Waleska and Marie-Louise of Austria. His most breathless moments in correspondence, however, he reserved for Josephine, as the following extracts testify:

★   I awake all filled with you. Your image and the intoxicating pleasures of last night, allow my senses no rest. Sweet and matchless Josephine, how strangely you work upon my heart … My soul is broken with grief and my love for you forbids repose … In three hours I shall see you again. Till then, a thousand kisses, mio dolce amor! But give me none back for they set my blood on fire.

★ Come soon; I warn you, if you delay, you will find me ill. Fatigue and your absence are too much … Your letters are the joy of my days, and my days of happiness are not many … A kiss on the heart, and one lower down, much lower!

★ Oh, my adorable wife! I don't know what fate has in store for me, but if it keeps me apart from you any longer, it will be unbearable! My courage is not enough for that …

★ Things are going well here; but my heart is indescribably heavy. You are ill and far away from me. Be gay and take great care of yourself, you are worth more than all the universe to me.

Medieval manual

An Italian manuscript, written in Latin on parchment, dating from the twelfth century gives advice on how to write love letters. The author of *Modi dictaminum* was a cleric called Guido, believed to come from Casentino on the border between Tuscany and Emilia. Its advice includes the following:

★   Always praise the beauty and qualities of the recipient. Use comparisons to famous couples (Paris and Helen, Pyramus and Thisbe etc) or similarities to precious stones.

★   Use phrases that indicate how impossible it is to describe the depth of your feeling: 'How deeply I love you I cannot express with words, even if all the members of my body could talk.'

★   Use apostrophic expressions: 'your beauty knows', 'your sweetness knows'; 'it is known to your nobility'.

★   Lament the distance between you with extreme lovesickness: 'The soul cannot stand much joy'.

★   Refer to the physical side of love: talk of hugs, kisses, desire, of 'sweet things to do together'.

Pet names

Britain's famous wartime Prime Minister Winston Churchill first met Clementine Hozier at a ball in London. He was thirty and an adventurer – a soldier, journalist and politician. She was just nineteen. They met again four years later in 1908 and were irresistibly drawn to one another. They married and then began a lifetime of lively and loving correspondence. In their letters, Clementine referred to herself as 'Kat' or 'Cat'; Winston was 'Pug' or 'Pig' and their children also received pet names. Their letters were often decorated with drawings and the subject matter ranged widely – not just concerning home and children, but also major political events.

Love on trial

In the spring of 1895 London hung on the three trials involving Oscar Wilde. Wilde had met and fallen in love with the young poet Lord Alfred Douglas ('Bosie') in 1891. Wilde had been blackmailed when a man called Alfred Wood found letters written by Wilde to Lord Alfred. But it was Douglas's father, John Sholto Douglas, who was instrumental in Wilde starting libel proceedings. Correspondence played a large role in the evidence introduced in court. Often highly suggestive,

Wilde was questioned regarding the homoerotic connotations of his letters.

Although this letter supports the case against Wilde, his lawyer introduced it to prevent the other side from using it in a more dramatic fashion later.

January 1893, Babbacombe Cliff

My Own Boy,

Your sonnet is quite lovely, and it is a marvel that those red-roseleaf lips of yours should be made no less for the madness of music and song than for the madness of kissing. Your slim gilt soul walks between passion and poetry. I know Hyacinthus, whom Apollo loved so madly, was you in Greek days. Why are you alone in London, and when do you go to Salisbury? Do go there to cool your hands in the grey twilight of Gothic things, and come here whenever you like. It is a lovely place and lacks only you; but go to Salisbury first.

Always, with undying love,

Yours, Oscar

Mystery letter

The following 200-year-old love letter was found in the arm of a chair at the premises of a furniture upholsterer in Gloucestershire, England. The note was tightly folded up to the size of a penny. Written in Old French, in pencil, it was composed from a man to a woman and sent from the town of Mercurol in the Alps. Nothing else is known about it or its lovers.

My dear small love, do not be worried, do you seriously believe I would tell anything to these people, who don't understand anything about love?

If someone insists that I say something, it will be anything but the dear love acquired by you, which is the great treasure hidden in my heart.

I didn't tell you to come yesterday because I didn't have the opportunity, but do come every Tuesday around 5.30, and Fridays as well; I count/hope on you tomorrow.

At the moment I write this letter, I can hear my aunt yelling, who else annoys us all day long, today and tomorrow.

300 love letters

In the early 2000s, Asia Wong from New Orleans decided to turn the idea of the love letter as something personal and singular on its head. She embarked on a project to write 300 letters and send them to strangers. There is something vaguely prurient about reading mail that is not intended for you, and Wong pushed the boundaries further by fixing each love note to the outside of the envelope so it could be read by anyone.

'Of course, it's about love, and relationships,' she says on her website www.sleeptrip.com. 'By the end of the project I wanted to be able to write a love letter to anyone, a stranger on the street, or someone that I have nothing but scorn for [...] I wanted to train my heart to really feel.'

The letters were colour-coordinated – for lovers, strangers, acquaintances, friends, etc. By the end, Wong had actually written a further 100 letters, feeling she hadn't quite accomplished her emotional journey when she fulfilled her original objective. Here are excerpt from two of her letters.

Letter to a crush

> My coffee's getting cold as I wait for you to show up. Will you, won't you, will you, won't you, won't you, won't you join the dance? I don't know you much, but I want to, I want to see you, feel your smile. I'm so close to leaping across, inappropriately, making a fool of myself, falling in love. I want to. Asia

Letter to a dream lover

> I'D LIKE TO SINK INTO YOU. And go to sleep for a GOOD, LONG While …
>
> Love, ASIA

The Love Letter Collection

The Love Letter Collection is an online and ongoing collection of anonymous love letters, which are submitted by the public. The project was started in 2001 by poet and artist Cynthia Gray and is made up of love letters that have been sent or received, as well as those the writer would like to send but can't. Letters are selected three times a year and published online at www.collectiveexperience.org. According to the website, 'the love can be a fantasy love, desperate love, unrequited love, impossible love, I love, frustrated love, absurd love, obsessed love, new love, fleeting love or love lost.' Here are some moving examples from the collection.

I felt and I honestly wanted:

> I've never met anyone like you. There was a spark and I thought your eyes were beautiful. I got home and wrote down how I felt and I honestly wanted to die for making a mistake that affected you.
>
> You are special. You had a huge effect on me. I was crying inside because it was impossible.

By the Lake:

My Dear _____

I want you to know that you gave me life again ... with those few brief meetings by the lake. I knew then that I could love again. I thought it would be, and I am so sorry it wasn't. I was planning our wedding day ... once again! I was thinking November would have been appropriate. I'll never regret that you looked me up after all those years.

You have no idea how you broke my heart when you told me you married her. But I owe you a huge Thanks ... for letting me know my heart wasn't dead. I hope your life is good and full of love and happiness. I have moved on. I actually think I'm in love again!

Thanks _____, you gave me my life back ... even if you aren't in it.

P.S. I still love you and always will.

On the Swings:

Today, when you sat next to me on the swings, did you ignore the tears in my eyes as you have ignored my being in love with you for so long?

PS, I Love You

Irish writer Cecelia Ahern's novel *P.S. I Love You* became a bestseller in 2004. In the book, a young woman, Holly Kennedy, is grieving after the death of Gerry, the love of her life. However, in the months before his death, Gerry wrote a series of ten letters to Holly, to guide her through her grief and into a new life without him. Each letter signs off in the same way: 'P.S. I Love You x'.

The novel was made into a movie, released in 2007, starring Hilary Swank and Gerard Butler.

A novel approach: letters in literature

I made a fire; being tired
Of the white fists of old
Letters and their death rattle
When I came too close to the wastebasket
What did they know that I didn't?

Sylvia Plath, 'Burning the Letters'

Many of the greatest contributors to literature were also prolific letter-writers. Those letters that have been preserved and published offer us an intimate encounter with a writer. While historically letter-writing was essential for communicating with friends and family members, correspondence was also a means of honing a writer's craft, of verbally sparing with their peers, and of expressing sentiments unique from those in their published writings.

Letters feature prominently in works of fiction, providing an alternative framework for characterization and relaying information. Some novels are made up entirely of letters.

How many letters?

In *The Oxford Book of Letters* (OUP, 1995) editors Frank and Anita Kermode point out that some letter-writers appear extraordinarily prolific. Their heavyweights include:

★ **G.B. SHAW** – 'tens of thousands' of letters extant.

★ **E.M. FORSTER** – 'about 11,000 letters survive'

★ **VIRGINIA WOOLF** – 'six big volumes'

★ **D.H. LAWRENCE** – 'seven volumes', despite dying when he was forty-four

★ **HORACE WALPOLE** – 'correspondence fills almost fifty volumes in the Yale edition'

However, the editors also suggest that 'Perhaps these totals are less extraordinary than they look; they will seem less amazing if one reflects that most of us write at least half a dozen letters of one sort or another every week, so that in the fifty or sixty years of a normal writing life many people must dispatch about 18,000 letters.'

The epistolary novel

An epistolary novel is a story told entirely through a series of letters. It is a style that was popularized in the eighteenth century by such writers as Samuel Richardson. Correspondence allows the writer to use the voice of the characters, offering more immediacy with the reader, which is difficult to achieve when writing solely in the third person.

Some definitions of the form also include diary entries, newspaper cuttings, emails and blogs. One theory runs that the genre originated from novels that just happened to have letters included as part of the text but that, over the years, the intervening narrative was gradually reduced. Another theory is that the form arose from miscellanies of letters and poetry, tied together into a plot.

Types of epistolary novels
There are various types of epistolary novel. Sometimes they can show just one point of view but often they are employed as a way to express several varying points of view and states of mind through simultaneous yet separate correspondences.

* Monologic – giving the letters of only one character. For example, *Letters of a Portuguese Nun*, attributed to Gabriel-Joseph de La Vergne (1669)

* Dialogic – giving the letters of two characters. For example, *Letters of Fanni Butlerd* (1757) by Mme Marie Jeanne Riccoboni

* Polylogic – letters from three or more characters. For example, *Clarissa* by Samuel Richardson (1749) and *Dangerous Liaisons* by Pierre Choderlos de Laclos (1782)

The letters of a Portuguese nun

Les Lettres Portugaises (traduites en françois) was first published anonymously in Paris in 1669 and became an instant publishing sensation. It was formed of five letters and controversy raged over the identity of the letter-writer, believed to be Portuguese and said to be a nun.

The letters are believed to be epistolary fiction and interest in them was so high in the seventeenth century that the word 'portugaise' become synonymous with 'a passionate love letter'. This extract reveals why.

> I conjure you to tell me wherefore you sought, as you did, to captivate my soul, since you well knew you were to leave me! And wherefore have you been so eager to make me unhappy? Why did you not leave me in the repose of my cloister? Had I done you any wrong?

> Yet pardon me, I impute nothing to you; I have no right to think of blame; I accuse only the severity of my fate: in separating us, it has inflicted all the evil that it could. It cannot separate our hearts; love, stronger than fate, has united them for ever: if my heart is still dear to you, write to me often. I surely merit that you should take some little pains to let me know the state of your heart, and of your fortune. Above all, come to see me.

Adieu! I know not how to quit this paper; it will fall into your hands. Would the same happiness were mine! Alas, senseless that I am! I well know that is not possible.

Adieu I can proceed no further.

Adieu; love me always, and be the cause of my enduring still severer sorrow.

Aphra Behn

Aphra Behn, one of the first female English professional writers, is also believed to have been one of the first to popularize the epistolary novel. Her work *Love-Letters Between a Nobleman and His Sister* was originally published as three separate volumes (in 1684, 1685 and 1687) and explores the events of the Monmouth Rebellion. Using *Les Lettres Portugaises* as a model, Behn also employed dramatic techniques allowing her to play with the reader's sense of reality and truth.

Behn paved the way for professional female writers to follow. Indeed, Virginia Woolf remarked, 'All women together ought to let flowers fall upon the tomb of Aphra Behn, for it was she who earned them the right to speak their minds.'

Popular eighteenth-century epistolary novels

Epitstolary fiction reached its heyday in the eighteenth century. The way in which the form enabled the reader a privileged peek into the psychology of the protagonists was a key device. Many believe it was essential to the development of the novel. Here are some of the most popular volumes of the day.

★ *Pamela* (1740), *Clarissa* (1749) and *The History of Sir Charles Grandison* (1753) by Samuel Richardson. In *Pamela* the letters are almost exclusively written by the namesake. In Richardson's other works, the outlook is widened.

★ *Lettres persanes* by Charles de Secondat, baron de Montesquieu, (1721) recounts the travels of two Persian noblemen, Usbek and Rica, through France.

★ *Julie, ou la nouvelle Heloise* by Jean-Jacques Rousseau (1761) – originally titled *Letters from two lovers living in a small town at the foot of the Alps.*

★ *Les Liaisons Dangereuses* by Choderlos de Laclos (1782) – the letters between protagonists Valmont and the Marquise drive the plot, although letters from other characters add depth.

★ *Die Leiden des jungen Werthers* (The Sorrows of Young Werther) by Johann Wolfgang von Goethe (1774). Loosely autobiographical novel, presented in the form of letters written by the artist Werther to his friend Wilhelm.

★ *Hyperion* by Friedrich Holderlin (1797–99). Set in Greece, the book comprises letters written by Hyperion to his friends Bellarmin and Diotima.

★ *The History of Emily Montague* by Frances Brooke (1769). Held to be the first Canadian novel, as Brooke, an Englishwoman by birth, was living in Quebec when she wrote it.

Modern epistolary novels

Although the popularity of the epistolary novel may have declined along with letter-writing itself, there have been some notable successes in recent years.

* *The Color Purple* by Alice Walker (1982) – set in rural Georgia, USA, during the 1930s, the novel received the 1983 Pulitzer Prize for Fiction and the National Book Award. It has been made into both a film and a musical. The protagonist, Celie, is a poor uneducated fourteen-year old black girl who writes letters to God.

* *The Guernsey Literary and Potato Peel Pie Society* by Mary Ann Shaffer (2008). Set in 1946 in the form of letters mainly to and from the central character, Juliet Ashton, a successful writer who becomes involved with a group of people on the island of Guernsey.

* *We Need to Talk about Kevin* by Lionel Shriver (2003) – monologic novel, written as a series of letters by Eva Khatchadourian to her husband, Franklin as she tries to come to terms with their son Kevin's killing spree. It won the 2005 Orange Prize and was recently made into a film starring Tilda Swinton.

★ *The Sorceror's House* by Gene Wolfe (2010) – fantasy novel written in the form of letters from the narrator to his brother.

★ *Clara Callan* by Richard B. Wright (2001) – letters and journal entries weave a story of self-discovery for the eponymous Clara living and loving in 1930s New York. It won the Governor-General's Award and the Giller Prize in Canada (where it was first published).

Postcards, stamps and prose

The *Griffin and Sabine Trilogy* is a series of three epistolary novels – *Griffin and Sabine* (1991), *Sabine's Notebook* (1992) and *The Golden Mean* (1993) – written by Nick Bantock. The story is told through a series of letters and postcards sent between the two eponymous characters, Griffin Moss (an artist in London who makes postcards) and Sabine Strohem (an artist living in the South Pacific who designs postage stamps). Each page shows a facsimile of a postcard or a letter inside an actual envelope, which can be removed to read.

Epistles in the Bible

The epistles in the Bible are divided into those of Paul and 'general' letters. The Epistles of Paul (otherwise known as the Pauline Epistles or Letters of Paul) are some of the earliest Christian documents still surviving. They constitute thirteen books in the New Testament and were directed to specific communities or congregations: Romans, First Corinthians, Second Corinthians, Galatians, Ephesians, Philippians, Colossians, First Thessalonians, Second Thessalonians, First Timothy, Second Timothy, Titus and Philemon. Some also include Hebrews but Paul's authorship is in question. Scholars still debate how many of the letters Paul actually wrote.

The General Epistles (also called the Catholic Epistles) were, it seems, directed to a Christian audience in general. They comprise (listed in the order they appear in the New Testament): the Epistle of James, the First Epistle of Peter, the Second Epistle of Peter, the First Epistle of John, the Second Epistle of John, the Third Epistle of John and the Epistle of Jude.

St Paul to the Corinthians

This letter is one of the most famous in the world, containing classic lines such as 'For now we see through a glass, darkly' and 'O death, where is thy sting?' Written in AD 54, its key theme is that people should love their fellow human beings – a universal, rather than erotic, love. Paul was aiming to lay down guidelines for the Christian community in Corinth. This extract is taken from the *New English Bible*, I Corinthians 13: 1–7.

> From Paul, apostle of Jesus Christ at God's call and by God's will together with our colleague Sosthenes, to the congregation of God's people at Corinth, dedicated to him in Christ Jesus, […] Grace and peace to you from God our Father and the Lord Jesus Christ.

> […] I may speak in tongues of men or of angels, but if I am without love, I am a sounding gong or a clanging cymbal. I may have the gift of prophecy, and know every hidden truth; I may have faith strong enough to move mountains; but if I have no love, I am nothing. I may dole out all I possess, or even give my body to be burned, but if I have no love, I am none the better:

Love is patient; love is kind and envies no one. Love is never boastful, nor conceited, nor rude; never selfish, not quick to take offense. Love keeps no score of wrongs; does not gloat over other men's sins, but delights in the truth. There is nothing love cannot face; there is no limit to its faith, its hope and its endurance.

[…] This greeting is in my own hand

PAUL.

Letters in horror novels

Frankenstein by Mary Shelley (1818). The story is presented through the letters of a sea captain and scientific explorer trying to reach the North Pole – he encounters Victor Frankenstein and records his dying confession.

Dracula by Bram Stoker (1897) is composed entirely of letters along with diary entries, newspaper cuttings, telegrams, ships' logs and doctors' notes.

Carrie by Stephen King (1974) is written using magazine articles, newspaper cuttings and excerpts from books and letters.

Some of Your Blood by Theodore Sturgeon (1961) is a short horror novel comprised of letters and case notes surrounding the treatment of a vampire.

The Historian by Elizabeth Kostova (2005) ties together three separate narratives all centred round the search for Vlad the Impaler's tomb, using a combination of letters and oral accounts.

Letters in Shakespeare

Shakespeare put letters in all but five of his plays; 111 letters appear on stage. The letters would have been sent by messengers – not to an address but to the specific person.

★   Letters feature heavily in *King Lear* – the word itself appears thirty-three times in the play. Letters are used to advance the plot, emphasize the main themes and to give insights into the characters.

★   In *Macbeth*, we first meet Lady Macbeth reading a letter. She also repeatedly writes and seals a letter in her sleep – we never discover the contents.

★   Three letters appear in *Romeo and Juliet*, the last being Romeo's suicide note to his father: 'Ay, but love cannot be controlled! To me, she is life, earth, and heaven itself, and without her, I would to my grave, to accompany her in her eternal sleep.'

★   In *Twelfth Night*, Maria and her friends plan to get their own back on Malvolio by forging a love letter from Olivia to Malvolio and appealing to his vanity.

★   In *As You Like It,* Phoebe writes a love letter to Ganymede (Rosalind disguised as a boy) and Silvius delivers it.

Letters to Juliet

Shakespeare's play *Romeo and Juliet* has inspired thousands of people to write love letters. The wall under Juliet's supposed balcony in Verona, Italy, is covered with small romantic notes. People believe that by leaving the letters, or even just writing their names and the name of their beloved on the wall itself, they will make their love everlasting.

Since the 1930s, people have also been writing letters to Juliet in Verona. More than 5,000 letters arrive each year – the largest group of senders being American teenagers. The letters have been read and replied to since the 1980s by a team of volunteers in the Club di Guilietta (Juliet Club), financed by the City of Verona. The 2006 work of non-fiction *Letters to Juliet* by Lise and Carl Friedman chronicles this phenomenon and inspired the 2010 romantic film of the same name starring Amanda Seyfried.

Possession

The winner of the Man Booker Prize for 1990, *Possession: A Romance* by A.S. Byatt, was also included by *Time* magazine in its TIME 100 Best English-language Novels from 1923 to 2005. The title refers, in part, to the collection of historically significant cultural works. The novel uses many different forms of written narrative, including diaries, letters and poetry (alongside standard third-person narration). Present-day academics Roland Michell and Maud Bailey follow a trail of clues from letters and journals to uncover the relationship between two fictional Victorian poets (Randolph Henry Ash and Christabel LaMotte).

Mark Twain – *Letters from the Earth*

The title of Mark Twain's posthumously published collection of short stories is taken from a story that consists of eleven letters written by Satan to the archangels Gabriel and Michael after he is banished (for a celestial day) to Earth. It was written shortly before Twain's death in 1909.

Satan's Letter

This is a strange place, an extraordinary place, and interesting. There is nothing resembling it at home. The people are all insane, the other animals are all insane, the earth is insane, Nature itself is insane. Man is a marvellous curiosity. When he is at his very very best he is a sort of low grade nickel-plated angel; at his worst he is unspeakable, unimaginable; and first and last and all the time he is a sarcasm. Yet he blandly and in all sincerity calls himself the 'noblest work of God.' This is the truth I am telling you. And this is not a new idea with him, he has talked it through all the ages, and believed it. Believed it, and found nobody among all his race to laugh at it.

The wit and wisdom of Jane Austen

Jane Austen loved letters. Her novella *Lady Susan* was written in an epistolary style, as were many of her juvenile writings. Some think that her lost novel *First Impressions* (which was redrafted to become *Pride and Prejudice*) may have been epistolary. *Pride and Prejudice* certainly contains a lot of letters quoted in full – some of which play a critical role in the plot.

She wrote hordes of personal letters and her characteristic wit shines through.

★ 'I do not want people to be very agreeable, as it saves me the trouble of liking them a lot.'

★ 'He seems a very harmless sort of young man, nothing to like or dislike in him – goes out shooting or hunting with the two others all the morning, and plays at whist and makes queer faces in the evening.'

★ 'I have read *The Corsair* [by Byron], mended my petticoat, and have nothing else to do.'

★ 'I believe I drank too much wine last night at Hurstbourne; I know not how else to account for the shaking of my hand to-day. You will kindly make allowance therefore for any indistinctness of writing, by attributing it to this venial error.'

★   'Poor woman! How can she honestly be breeding again?'

The great age of letter-writing lies in the past

'One thing seems certain and sad enough: the number of future claimants for representation in such a collection as this is not going to grow very quickly. The great age of letter-writing was, roughly, 1700–1918. Of course there are many good letters after that – think only of D.H. Lawrence and Virginia Woolf – and as Yeats remarked, thinking of poetry, though the great song is heard no more there's a keen delight in what we have. But by the time of the Second World War there were a lot of those telephones about, admittedly less handy than they are now; and the postal service had begun to shrink and slow down ...'

– *Frank and Anita Kermode, in the introduction to* The Oxford Book of Letters.

Until we meet again: farewell letters

If you knew death was approaching and you had one last chance to write a letter to your loved ones, what would it say? A heartbreaking situation, but one that has been faced by many men and women throughout history, whether on the battlefield, lying in a hospital bed or awaiting the final throes of illness. Some of the letters in this chapter are agonizing to read, some hopeful, some plaintive, but all of them reveal that, in the final moments, we write naturally, honestly and with great clarity of feeling.

Awaiting execution

Days or hours before their executions, these historical figures penned letters to family members or religious leaders saying offering farewells, begging for mercy or beseeching pardon.

Sir Thomas More to Margaret Roper (1535)

More was executed the day after writing this letter to his daughter:

> Our Lord bless you, good daughter, and your good husband, and your little boy, and all yours, and all my children, and all my godchildren and all our friends. Recommend me when ye may to my good daughter Cicely, whom I beseech our Lord to comfort .... For it is Saint Thomas' even and the Utas of Saint Peter; and therefore tomorrow long I to go to God: it were a day very meet and convenient for me ... Farewell, my dear child, and pray for me, and I shall for you and all your friends, that we may merrily meet in Heaven ...

Catherine of Aragon to Henry VIII (1535)

My Lord and Dear Husband, I commend me unto you. The hour of my death draweth fast on, and my case being such, the tender love I owe you forceth me, with a few words, to put you in remembrance of the health and safeguard of your soul, which you ought to prefer before all worldly matters, and before the care and tendering of your own body, for the which you have cast me into many miseries and yourself into many cares.

For my part I do pardon you all, yea, I do wish and devoutly pray God that He will also pardon you ...

Mary Queen of Scots to Pope Sixtus V (1586)

Now, Holy Father, it hath pleased God to allow, because of my sins and those of the people of this unfortunate island, that after 20 years of imprisonment, I (the sole descendant of the house of England and Scotland to profess this faith) be shut up in a narrow prison and finally condemned by the ... heretical assembly of this country to die.

Sir Walter Raleigh to Elizabeth Raleigh (1603)
Despite this letter, Ralegh was not actually executed until 1618.

> You shall now receive (my deare wife) my last words in these my last lines. My love that I send you that you may keep it when I am dead, and my councell that you may remember it when I am no more. I would not by my will present you with sorrowes (dear Besse) let them go to the grave with me and be buried in the dust. And seeing that it is not Gods will that I should see you any more in this life, beare it patiently, and with a heart like they selfe …

Marie Antoinette to her sister-in-law Elizabeth (1793)

This letter was penned hours before Marie was taken to the guillotine.

My sister, I am writing to you for the very last time: I have just been condemned to a death that is in no way shameful – since a shameful death is a fate reserved for criminals – but I am going on a journey to meet your brother once again. I hope I will show the same fortitude as he in my last moments.

I am calm, as one always is when one's conscience is clear. I am deeply saddened to abandon my children: you know that I have lived for them alone ...

Letter from the battlefield

Johannes Haas wrote to his parents from Verdun in 1916: 'Dear Parents, I am lying on the battlefield, wounded in the body. I think I am dying. I am glad to have time to prepare for the heavenly homecoming. Thank you dear parents. God be with you. Hans.'

A final love letter

The Union soldier Sullivan Ballou wrote to his wife, Sarah Hart Shumway, on 14 July 1861, one week before he was killed at the First Battle of Bull Run, the first major land battle of the American Civil War. It is uncertain whether the letter was ever posted: it was found in Major Ballou's trunk after his death and was delivered to his widow by Governor William Sprague. Below is a moving extract:

> Sarah, my love for you is deathless, it seems to bind me with mighty cables that nothing but omnipotence can break; and yet my love of Country comes over me like a strong wind and bears me irresistibly with all those chains to the battlefield. The memory of all the blissful moments I have enjoyed with you come crowding over me, and I feel most deeply grateful to God and you, that I have enjoyed them for so long. And how hard it is for me to give them up and burn to ashes the hopes and future years, when, God willing, we might still have lived and loved together, and see our boys grown up to honorable manhood around us. If I do not return, my dear Sarah, never forget how much I loved you, nor that when my last breath escapes me on the battle field, it will whisper

your name ... Forgive my many faults, and the many pains I have caused you. How thoughtless, how foolish I have sometimes been!

Postscript from a dying man

Captain Robert Falcon Scott (Scott 'of the Antarctic') wrote seven letters to friends and family as he lay dying at the end of his successful but doomed expedition to the South Pole. J.M. Barrie, Scott's friend and godfather to his son, Peter, was one of the recipients. Barrie was so touched by the letter that he carried it with him for the rest of his life. This is its postscript:

> We are in a desperate state, feet frozen, etc. No fuel and a long way from food, but it would do your heart good to be in our tent, to hear our songs and the cheery conversation as to what we will do when we get to Hut Point.
>
> Later ... We are very near the end, but have not and will not lose our good cheer. We have had four days of storm in our tent and nowhere's food or fuel. We did intend to finish ourselves when things proved like this, but we have decided to die naturally in the track.

As a dying man, my dear friend, be good to my wife and child. Give the boy a chance in life if the State won't do it. He ought to have good stuff in him … I never met a man in my life whom I admired and loved more than you, but I never could show you how much your friendship meant to me, for you had much to give and I nothing.

Letters to the dead

It seems likely that writing letters to relatives who had recently died was a common custom in ancient Egypt (2686–1069 BC). Around fifteen letters survive, most found in or around tombs. Generally they are inscribed on bowls, although some are written on papyrus or linen.

The dead were seen as powerful in ancient Egypt and it was believed that an angry or vengeful spirit could be responsible for the ill fortunes of the living. The purpose of the letters was to convince the dead that the writer treated them well during their life, despite any problems they may have shared, and so deserved intercession in the afterlife. Problems cited range from general ill health and weakness to disputes over money and property.

This letter was found inscribed on a pottery bowl and was written by a widow appealing for help for her daughter:

> A sister speaks to her brother. The sole friend Nefersefkhi. A great cry of grief! To whom is a cry of grief useful? You have given it for the crimes committed against my daughter evilly, evilly, though I have done nothing against him, nor have I consumed his property. He has not given anything to my daughter. Voice offerings are made to the spirit in return for watching over the earthly survivor. Make you your reckoning with whoever is doing what is painful to me, because my voice is true against any dead man or any dead woman who is doing these things against my daughter.

A postscript, usually abbreviated to PS, is a message appended at the end of a letter or other written communication. The phrase comes from the Latin *post scriptum*, meaning 'that which comes after the writing' and is often added as a hasty afterthought. With the rise in word processing, the postscript ought to be avoidable, but it may be used for effect rather than necessity, i.e. to reinforce a point already made, or for humour. A PS can frequently be the most telling part of a letter, written less self-consciously than the main body of text. You should refrain from using postscripts in formal letters.

Here are some examples from letter-writers of note:

★ HENRY MILLER to LAWRENCE DURRELL:
'PS Larry old boy … [Bill Pickerill] may find a
way of showing you the last watercolours I did
which he photographed in colour. I hope so –
they're the works of a dying man. That's about
it, Larry. All the best. Henry.'

★ JOHN KEATS to FANNY BRAWNE:
'PS Do not accuse me of delay – we have not
here an opportunity of sending letters every day.
Write speedily.'

★ NAPOLEON BONAPARTE to JOSEPHINE:
'PS – The war this year has changed beyond
recognition … . My soldiers are showing
inexpressible confidence in me; you alone are a
source of chagrin to me; you alone are the joy
and torment of my life … Woman!!!!'

★ CLEMENTINE CHURCHILL to WINSTON:
'PS Please be a good Pug and not destroy the
good of your little open air holiday by smoking
too many fat cigars.'

★ Horace **WALPOLE:**
'PS What is the history of the theatres this winter?'

★ **GEORGE BERNARD SHAW:**
'PS On your life, don't tell anybody.'

Bibliography and Sources

Alex, Ben, *Best Regards: Recovering the Art of Soulful Letter Writing* (Scandinavia Publishing House, 2003)

Blumenthal, Lassor, *The Art of Letter Writing* (Putnam Pub Group Library, 1976)

Decke, William Merrill, *Epistolary Practices: Letter Writing in America before Telecommunications* (University of North Carolina Press, 1998)

Fraser, Antonia (ed.), *Love Letters: An Illustrated Anthology* (Crescent Books, 1995)

Heller, Bernard, *The 100 Most Difficult Business Letters You'll Ever Have to Write, Fax or Email* (HarperBusiness, 1994)

Holland, Merlin and Hart-Davis, Rupert (eds), *The Complete Letters of Oscar Wilde* (Fourth Estate, 2000)

Kenyon, Olga, *800 Years of Women's Letters* (Sutton Publishing Ltd, 2003)

Kermode, Frank and Anita (eds), *The Oxford Book of Letters* (OUP, 2003)

King, Martin Luther, Jr., *Letter from the Birmingham Jail* (HarperCollins, 1994)

Klauser, Henriette Anne, *Put your Heart on Paper* (Bantam USA, 1995)

MacNiven, Ian (ed.), *The Durrell-Miller Letters, 1935-80* (Faber and Faber, 1988)

Maggi, Rosalie, *Great Letters for Every Occasion* (Prentice Hall, 1999)

Meyer, Harold E., *Lifetime Encyclopedia of Letters* (NYIF, 1991)

O'Sullivan, Vincent and Scott, Margaret (eds), *The Collected Letters of Katherine Mansfield: Volume IV: 1920–1921* (Clarendon Press, 1996)

Peterson, Merrill D. (ed.), *The Portable Thomas Jefferson* (Penguin, 1977)

Pool, Gail (ed.), *Other People's Mail: An Anthology of Letter Stories* (University of Missouri Press, 1999)

Powers, Lyall H.(ed.), *Henry James and Edith Wharton: Letters: 1900–1915* (Scribner, 1990)

Schuster, Lincoln M. (ed.), *The Treasury of the World's Great Letters: From Ancient Days to Our own Time* (Simon & Schuster, 1960)

Twain, Mark, *Letters from the Earth* (Harper Perennial, 2004)

Washington, Peter *Love Letters* (Everyman, 1996)

Williams, Jennifer, *The Pleasures of Staying in Touch: Writing Memorable Letters* (William Morrow & Company, 1998)

www.lettersofnote.com

www.sleeptrip.com

www.stevencurtis.com

Page 41: Robin Flies Again: Letters Written by women of Goucher College, class of 1903, http://meyerhoff.goucher.edu/library/robin/

Page 58: Letter to Laura Waugh dated 7 January 1945 by Evelyn Waugh. Copyright © The Estate of Laura Waugh, 1980, used by permission of The Wylie Agency (UK) Limited

Pages 120–2: *Lion Feuchtwanger an Bewohner seines Hause: Offener Brief an die Bewohner meines Hauses Mahlerstr. 8 in Berlin. In: Pariser Tageblatt 463, 20.3.1935.* © Aufbau Verlag GmbH & Co. KG, Berlin 1999

Pages 126–7: Courtesy of the Albert Einstein Archives, The Hebrew University of Jerusalem

Page 148: Letter from Oscar Wilde to Lord Alfred Douglas, in Merlin Holland and Rupert Hart-Davis (eds) *The Complete Letters of Oscar Wilde* © Merlin Holland 2000

Pages 152–3: Letters reproduced by kind permission of Cynthia Gray, www.collectiveexperience.org

Page 172: Extract from *Letters from the Earth* by Mark Twain © by Richard A. Watson and J.P. Morgan Chase Manhattan Bank as trustees of the Mark Twain Foundation

Pages 180–1: Ballou, Sullivan. Copy of a letter by Sullivan Ballou to his wife Sarah [transcriber unknown], 14 July 1861 [date of copy unknown, 19th c.], Sullivan Ballou Papers, MSS 277, Box 1, Folder 10, the Rhode Island Historical Society.

Index

C